Power UP

Power UP

A Practical Student's Guide to Online Learning

edition
2

STACEY BARRETT

CATRINA POE

CARRIE SPAGNOLA-DOYLE

PEARSON

Boston   Columbus   Indianapolis   New York   San Francisco   Upper Saddle River
Amsterdam   Cape Town   Dubai   London   Madrid   Milan   Munich   Paris   Montreal   Toronto
Delhi   Mexico City   Sao Paulo   Sydney   Hong Kong   Seoul   Singapore   Taipei   Tokyo

VP/Editor in Chief Student Success & Career Development: Jodi McPherson
Acquisitions Editor: Katie Mahan
Editorial Assistant: Clara Ciminelli
Executive Marketing Manager: Amy Judd
Production Editor: Karen Mason
Production Coordination and Electronic Composition: Cenveo Publisher Services/Nesbitt Graphics, Inc.
Text Design and Illustrations: Cenveo Publisher Services/Nesbitt Graphics, Inc.
Cover Designer: Diane Lorenzo
Chapter Illustrations: Danielle Couch
Colorizing Illustrations: Pearson Imaging Centers, Corin Skidds
Cover Photo: John Foxx/Stockbyte/Getty Images
Interior Photos: p. v, Connie Westpfahl; all other interior photos are from Shutterstock.com
Printer: Courier, Kendallville

Many of the designations by manufacturers and sellers to distinguish their products are claimed as trademarks. Where those designations appear in this book, and the publisher was aware of a trademark claim, the designations have been printed in initial caps or all caps.

Between the time website information is gathered and then published, it is not unusual for some sites to have closed. Also, the transcription of URLs can result in typographical errors. The publisher would appreciate notification where these errors occur so that they may be corrected in subsequent editions.

Library of Congress Cataloging-in-Publication Data

Barrett, Stacey.
 Power up : a practical student's guide to online learning / Stacey Barrett, Catrina Poe, Carrie Spagnola-Doyle. -- 2nd ed.
   p. cm.
 Includes bibliographical references and index.
 ISBN-13: 978-0-13-278819-9 (pbk.)
 ISBN-10: 0-13-278819-5 (pbk.)
 1. Computer-assisted instruction. 2. Education--Computer network resources. 3. Internet in education. I. Poe, Catrina. II. Spagnola-Doyle, Carrie. III. Title.
 LB1028.5.B357 2012
 371.33'44678--dc23

                    2011029590

V011
10 9 8

ISBN 10: 0-13-278819-5
ISBN 13: 978-0-13-278819-9

Authors Carrie Spagnola-Doyle, Catrina Poe, and Stacey Barrett

Carrie Spagnola-Doyle is Vice President of Curriculum and Instruction for Pearson Learning Solutions (PLS) and leads a group called PLS-CC, whose primary focus is the analysis, design, development, and evaluation of custom curriculum in all modalities. PLS-CC manages educational initiatives and creates solutions for higher education within the private sector, community colleges, state schools, k–12, government, associations, and corporations. She has been an approved online adjunct faculty member for University of Phoenix since 2003 and published her first book, *Journal to Fulfillment,* in 2002. Carrie holds a master's in business administration and bachelor of arts in communication. She lives in Queen Creek, Arizona, with her husband, Brian, daughter, Marlie, and their dog, Patches.

Catrina Poe is the Assistant Vice President of Academics for Pearson Learning Solutions. With over 20 years of experience in the educational industry, she has worked as an administrator as well as a faculty member. She started teaching online in the late 1990s. She holds a doctorate in business administration, and her dissertation was focused on implementing online programs at for-profit, career colleges. She is married with four children and lives in Mesa, Arizona.

Stacey Barrett is Director of Assessment and Learning for Pearson Learning Solutions. She has worked in higher education for over 15 years, specializing in the design of curriculum and assessments. Stacey holds a master's degree in learning and instructional technology. She lives in Chandler, Arizona.

BRIEF CONTENTS

CONTENTS

PART IV   TOOLS AND WORKSPACE

MISSION OF THE BOOK

Some research indicates that the majority of online students do not persist in their programs. They may drop out because they have misconceptions and/or misunderstandings regarding the realities of online learning including the expectations, the potential obstacles, and the necessary preparation required to succeed in the virtual classroom.

As an online student, you are embarking on a dream, making an investment in yourself, and reaching for success. This book is designed to support you as a student new to online learning by giving you practical tips and information to help you achieve your goals in the online environment efficiently and effectively.

NEW TO THIS EDITION

What makes this book a valuable resource to online learners is also the factor that necessitates frequent updates to its content: technology and culture are constantly evolving, and so aspects of online learning continue to change. In this second edition, we have updated the book in several ways:

- *Adding Sections:* Brief sections on the topics of mobile learning and new Learning Management Systems (LMS) options have been added to the appropriate chapters.
- *Adding Chapters:* Three areas are important enough to warrant the addition of completely new chapters in this edition—21ST-century skills, hybrid courses, and e-books.
- *Updating Content:* Throughout the book components such as research statistics and websites have been refreshed.
- *Adding Accessibility:* The text now has a new, easier-to-reference format.

ELEMENTS TO SUPPORT YOU

In this helpful guidebook, you will explore the realities of taking classes online. The material covers standard topics with an online spin, as well as these specific topics particularly relevant to online learners:

- Motivation
- Time management
- Self-knowledge, including learning styles
- The online classroom and community
- Working in the online classroom
- Communicating online
- Strategies for successful online learning
- Critical thinking and online research
- Leveraging e-books
- Computer concerns
- Creating a personalized study environment
- Maintaining online success

To help you focus your learning, a *Power UP* section begins each chapter, summarizing the important concepts. To expand your knowledge, a *More Power to You* section closes each chapter, listing websites that feature further information or ideas related to the material discussed in the chapter.

NEW! COURSESMART eTEXTBOOK AVAILABLE

 CourseSmart is an exciting new choice for students looking to save money. As an alternative to purchasing the printed textbook, students can purchase an electronic version of the same content. With a CourseSmart eTextbook, students can search the text, make notes online, print out reading assignments that incorporate lecture notes, and bookmark important passages for later review. For more information, or to purchase access to the CourseSmart eTextbook, visit www.coursesmart.com.

ELEMENTS INSTRUCTORS WILL FIND HELPFUL

This book is a resource to help students acclimate to the online classroom faster and more confidently than they would otherwise. As an added plus, instructors will find the information useful when conducting the online class. The available PowerPoint slides summarize the course concepts and provide an easy way for instructors to integrate concepts from the text into their classrooms.

ADDITIONAL RESOURCES FOR STUDENTS AND FACULTY

CourseConnect™

Ready for a complete, economical, and customizable online education solution? CODiE Award–winning *CourseConnect* features:

- A library of online courses created by respected subject matter experts and e-learning instructional designers
- Online course content based directly on clear learning objectives
- Recommendations of Pearson texts for each online course, but courses are customizable and work with any text
- Free comprehensive instructor's guide with each online course
- Online courses that work in any learning management system

 An associated *Student Success* course, which can be used in tandem with this text, is available from *Pearson's CourseConnect* library (www.pearsoncourseconnect.com). It provides a complete customizable curriculum in support of the concepts from this text and more.

SmarterMeasure℠

 The SmarterMeasure™ (www.SmarterMeasure.com) is an online assessment that helps you evaluate your strengths and opportunities for improvement in regards to learning online. It measures many of the items you have read about in this book so far. It helps you go into the online learning experience with your eyes wide open by helping you to understand your traits, attributes, and skills as well as what to expect in an online learning experience. SmarterMeasure will help you understand your readiness for online learning in the following areas:

- *Individual attributes.* How motivated are you? To what degree are you a procrastinator. Are you willing to ask for help when you need it?
- *Life factors.* How much time do you have to devote to online learning? Do you have support from family and your employer? Do you have a dedicated place for studying online?

- *Learning styles.* How do you learn best? Some students learn best alone, and other learn best surrounded by people. Some people learn best by reading, others by looking at pictures.
- *Technical competency.* How well can you use the computer, the Internet, and other forms of technology such as smartphones.
- *On-screen reading rate and recall.* How fast do you read from your computer screen, and how much of it do you remember?
- *Typing rate and accuracy.* How quickly and accurately do you type?

SmarterMeasure is a relatively simple way to explore how comfortable you will be with online education. There are no right and wrong answers. After you complete the assessment you will receive a score report that will help you understand what you can do to become a successful online learner. In addition to your score report, your school may also provide some additional resources to help you succeed.

ThinkWatson

To learn more about your personal thinking style, go to www.ThinkWatson.com/MyThinkingStyle and complete the "**My Thinking Style**" assessment.

There are seven positive styles—take the assessment and learn your strengths:

- Analytical: planful, orderly, methodical
- Inquisitive: curious, alert, interested in the surrounding world
- Insightful: prudent, humble, reflective
- Open-minded: empathic, tolerant of others, fair-minded
- Systematic: strategic, process-oriented, sees big picture
- Timely: efficient, reliable, resourceful
- Truth-seeking: independent, tough-minded, skeptical

ACKNOWLEDGMENTS

We would like to acknowledge first and foremost our families, for allowing us to dedicate the time to write this book.

Each of us would like to thank the other two for the opportunity to work as an author on this team.

We also would like to offer special recognition to the following individuals who helped us with various aspects of the book: Joe Spagnola, Lorenzo Sierra, danielle Couch, Dr. Nancy Forrester, Dr. James Wood, Dr. Pam Lawhead and the IAEGS Team, and Jesse Ong from Hallmark Institute of Technology.

And, our sincere thanks to the following reviewers:

Mac Adkins, DECADE Consulting/Troy University; Lisa Dodson, ECPI College of Technology; Dr. Nancy G. Forrester; Elaine Gray, Appalachian State University; Je'Loni Hall, Vatterott Educational Centers, Inc.; Lauren Hensley, Dennis Learning Center; Sheryl LaCoursiere, UMASS Boston; Noah Larsen, University of Colorado at Boulder; Dr. Pamela Lawhead, The University of Mississippi; Dr. Jamie Morley, Apollo College; Angela Oleson, independent online instructor; Dr. Bill Prado, Green Mountain College; Barbara Purvis, Centura College; Katie Rosenthal, Ashford University; Carole Suihkonen; Melissa Wertz, Pittsburg Technical Institute; and Dr. James M. Wood, University of Phoenix/Green Mountain College.

Supplemental Resources

INSTRUCTOR SUPPORT – Resources to simplify your life and support your students.

<u>Book Specific</u>

Online Instructor's Manual – This manual is intended to give professors a framework or blueprint of ideas and suggestions that may assist them in providing their students with activities, journal writing, thought-provoking situations, and group activities. The test bank, organized by chapter includes: multiple choice, true/false and short-answer questions that support the key features in the book. This supplement is available for download from the Instructor's Resource Center at www.pearsonhighered.com/irc

Online PowerPoint Presentation – A comprehensive set of PowerPoint slides that can be used by instructors for class presentations or by students for lecture preview or review. The PowerPoint Presentation includes bullet point slides for each chapter, as well as all of the graphs and tables found in the textbook. These slides highlight the important points of each chapter to help students understand the concepts within each chapter. Instructors may download these PowerPoint presentations from the Instructor's Resource Center at www .pearsonhighered.com/irc
'Inspiring you to inspire them.'

MyStudentSuccessLab – Are you teaching online, in a hybrid setting, or looking to infuse technology into your classroom for the first time? It is an online solution designed to help students build the skills they need to succeed for ongoing personal and professional development at www.mystudentsuccesslab.com

Other Resources

"Easy access to online, book-specific teaching support is now just a click away!"
Instructor Resource Center – Register. Redeem. Login. Three easy steps that open the door to a variety of print and media resources in downloadable, digital format, available to instructors exclusively through the Pearson 'IRC'. www.pearsonhighered.com/irc

"Provide information highlights on the most critical topics for student success!"
Success Tips is a 6-panel laminate with topics that include MyStudentSuccessLab, Time Management, Resources All Around You, Now You're Thinking, Maintaining Your Financial Sanity, and Building Your Professional Image. Other choices are available upon request.
This essential supplement can be packaged with any student success text to add value with 'just in time' information for students.

"Infuse student success into any program with our "IDentity" Series booklets!" - Written by national subject matter experts, the material contains strategies and activities for immediate application. Choices include:
- Financial Literacy (Farnoosh Torabi)
- Financial Responsibility (Clearpoint Financial)
- Now You're Thinking about Student Success (Judy Chartrand et.al.)
- Now You're Thinking about Career Success (Judy Chartrand et.al.)
- Ownership (Megan Stone)
- Critical Thinking: A Career Choice (Paul Schuler)
- Identity (Stedman Graham).

"Through partnership opportunities, we offer a variety of assessment options!"
LASSI – The LASSI is a 10-scale, 80-item assessment of students' awareness about and use of learning and study strategies. Addressing skill, will and self-regulation, the focus is on both covert and overt thoughts, behaviors, attitudes and beliefs that relate to successful learning and that can be altered through educational interventions. Available in two formats: Paper ISBN: 0131723154 or Online ISBN: 0131723162 (access card).

Noel Levitz/RMS – This retention tool measures Academic Motivation, General Coping Ability, Receptivity to Support Services, PLUS Social Motivation. It helps identify at-risk students, the areas with which they struggle, and their receptiveness to support. Available in paper or online formats, as well as short and long versions. Paper Long Form A: ISBN: 0135120667; Paper Short Form B: ISBN: 0135120659; Online Forms A,B & C: ISBN: 0130981583.

Robbins Self Assessment Library – This compilation teaches students to create a portfolio of skills. S.A.L. is a self-contained, interactive, library of 49 behavioral questionnaires that help students discover new ideas about themselves, their attitudes, and their personal strengths and weaknesses. Available in Paper, CD-Rom, and Online (Access Card) formats.

Supplemental Resources

Other Resources

"For a truly tailored solution that fosters campus connections and increases retention, talk with us about custom publishing."
Pearson Custom Publishing – We are the largest custom provider for print and media shaped to your course's needs.
Please visit us at www.pearsoncustom.com to learn more.

STUDENT SUPPORT – Tools to help make the grade now, and excel in school later.

"Now there's a Smart way for students to save money."
CourseSmart is an exciting new choice for students looking to save money. As an alternative to purchasing the printed textbook, students can purchase an electronic version of the same content. With a CourseSmart eTextbook, students can search the text, make notes online, print out reading assignments that incorporate lecture notes, and bookmark important passages for later review. For more information, or to purchase access to the CourseSmart eTextbook, visit www.coursesmart.com

"Today's students are more inclined than ever to use technology to enhance their learning."
MyStudentSuccessLab will engage students through relevant YouTube videos with 'how to' videos selected 'by students, for students' and help build the skills they need to succeed for ongoing personal and professional development. www.mystudentsuccesslab.com

"Time management is the #1 challenge students face."
Premier Annual Planner - This specially designed, annual 4-color collegiate planner includes an academic planning/resources section, monthly planning section (2 pages/month), weekly planning section (48 weeks; July start date), which facilitate short-term as well as long term planning. Spiral bound, 6x9.

"Journaling activities promote self-discovery and self-awareness."
Student Reflection Journal - Through this vehicle, students are encouraged to track their progress and share their insights, thoughts, and concerns. 8 1/2 x 11. 90 pages.

MyStudentSuccessLab

Start Strong. Finish Stronger.
www.MyStudentSuccessLab.com

MyStudentSuccessLab is an online solution designed to help students acquire the skills they need to succeed for ongoing personal and professional development. They will have access to peer-led video interviews and develop core skills through interactive practice exercises and activities that provide academic, life, and professional skills that will transfer to ANY course.

It can accompany any Student Success text or can be used as a stand-alone course offering.

How will MyStudentSuccessLab make a difference?

Is motivation a challenge, and if so, how do you deal with it?

Video Interviews – Experience peer led video 'by students, for students' of all ages and stages.

How would better class preparation improve the learning experience?

Practice Exercises – Practice skills for each topic—leveled by Bloom's taxonomy.

What could you gain by building critical thinking and problem-solving skills?

Activities – Apply what is being learned to create 'personally relevant' resources through enhanced communication and self-reflection.

MyStudentSuccessLab

Start Strong. Finish Stronger.
www.MyStudentSuccessLab.com

As an instructor, how much easier would it be to assign and assess on MyStudentSuccessLab if you had a Learning Path Diagnostic that reported to the grade book?

Learning Path Diagnostic

- For the **course**, 65 Pre-Course questions (Levels I & II Bloom's) and 65 Post-Course questions (Levels III & IV Bloom's) that link to key learning objectives in each topic.

- For each **topic**, 20 Pre-Test questions (Levels I & II Bloom's) and 20 Post-Test questions (Levels III & IV Bloom's) that link to all learning objectives in the topic.

As a student, how much more engaged would you be if you had access to relevant YouTube videos within MyStudentSuccessLab?

Student Resources

A wealth of resources like our FinishStrong247 YouTube channel with 'just in time' videos selected 'by students, for students.'

MyStudentSuccessLab Topic List:

1. A First Step: Goal Setting
2. Communication
3. Critical Thinking
4. Financial Literacy
5. Information Literacy

6. Learning Preferences
7. Listening and Taking Notes in Class
8. Majors and Careers
9. Memory and Studying
10. Problem Solving

11. Professionalism
12. Reading and Annotating
13. Stress Management
14. Test Taking Skills
15. Time Management

MyStudentSuccessLab Feature set:

Learning Path Diagnostic: 65 Pre-Course (Levels I & II Bloom's) and 65 Post-Course (Levels III & IV Bloom's) / Pre-Test (Levels I & II Bloom's) and Post-Test (Levels III & IV Bloom's).

Topic Overview: Module objectives.

Video Interviews: Real video interviews 'by students, for students' on key issues.

Practice Exercises: Skill-building exercises per topic provide interactive experience and practice.

Activities: Apply what is being learned to create 'personally relevant' resources through enhanced communication and self-reflection.

Student Resources: Pearson Students Facebook page, FinishStrong247 YouTube channel, MySearchLab, Online Dictionary, Plagiarism Guide, Student Planner, and Student Reflection Journal.

Implementation Guide: Grading rubric to support instruction with Overview, Time on Task, suggested grading, etc.

PEARSON

Pearson Success Tips, 1/e

ISBN-10: 0132788071 • ISBN-13: 9780132788076

Success Tips is a 6-panel laminate that provides students with information highlights on the most critical topics for student success. These topics include MyStudentSuccessLab, Time Management, Resources All Around You, Now You're Thinking, Maintaining Your Financial Sanity, and Building Your Professional Image. Other choices are available upon request via our www.pearsoncustomlibrary.com program, as well as traditional custom publishing. This essential supplement can be packaged with any student success text to add value with 'just in time' information for students.

Features

- **MyStudentSuccessLab** - Helps students 'Start strong, Finish stronger' by getting the most out of this technology with their book.
- **Time Management** - Everyone begins with the same 24 hours in the day, but how well students use their time varies.
- **Resources All Around You** - Builds awareness for the types of resources available on campus of which students can take advantage.
- **Now You're Thinking** - Learning to think critically is imperative to student success.
- **Maintaining Your Financial Sanity** - Paying attention to savings, spending, and borrowing choices is more important than ever.
- **Building Your Professional Image** - Students are motivated by preparing for their future careers through online and in person professional tips, self-branding, and image tips.
- **Additional Topics** - Other choices are available upon request via our www.pearsoncustomlibrary.com program, as well as traditional custom publishing. This essential supplement can be packaged with any student success text to add value with 'just in time' information for students.

Topic List

- MyStudentSuccessLab*
- Time Management*
- Resources All Around You*
- Now You're Thinking*
- Maintaining Your Financial Sanity*
- Building Your Professional Image*
- Get Ready for Workplace Success
- Civility Paves the Way Toward Success

- Succeeding in Your Diverse World
- Information Literacy is Essential to Success
- Protect Your Personal Data
- Create Your Personal Brand
- Service Learning
- Stay Well and Manage Stress
- Get Things Done with Virtual Teams
- Welcome to Blackboard!

- Welcome to Moodle!
- Welcome to eCollege!
- Set and Achieve Your Goals
- Prepare for Test Success
- Good Notes Are Your Best Study Tool
- Veterans/Military Returning Students

NOTE: those with asterisks are 'default' options; topic selection can be made through Pearson Custom Library at www.pearsoncustomlibrary.com, as well as traditional custom publishing.

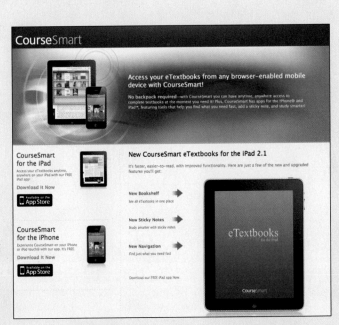

📶 LOOKING AT ONLINE LEARNING

Many students begin an online program and wonder if they made the best decision. Some call this "buyer's remorse"; others may say they suffer from "cognitive dissonance." The bottom line: It is a scary new adventure and you may have a lot of questions. You have taken the plunge. You are an online learner! This book will help you through the experience. We answer many of the questions that being an online learner presents—questions you may already have as well as questions you may not have thought to ask yet. We also provide tips for success based on our own experiences and the experiences of our students.

Students are often faced with questions like these: "Is your school a real university?" "How can you learn online?" "Are you sure your degree will be worth anything?" or the famous "Do employers hire people with an online education?" Of course companies hire people with degrees received from an online institution, and, yes, your degree can be a worthwhile investment. There is a misconception that online education is the "easy route" and degrees garnered in this modality are not really "earned," but we assure you (and we know students who have been through an online program will attest to this, too) nothing could be further from the truth.

In this book, we identify, discuss, and dispel these and numerous other myths regarding online education. However, to begin, we want to arm you with some knowledge that will help you address these questions and any doubts you may have about online education.

The number of students enrolled in online education programs is growing rapidly. The number of students taking some classes online was approximately 6 million in 2010, an increase of 1 million more students as compared to 2009 (Allen & Seaman, 2010). Some experts predict this number will be 21.13 million in 2015. Keep in mind, in 2010, there were about 20 million students in postsecondary programs. Further, students taking their entire program online will grow from 1.37 million in 2011 to 3.86 million in 2015. If the trend continues, by the year 2018 there will be more students taking classes and programs online than on ground (Nagel, 2011).

In addition, many high schools are now moving toward offering online options. According to Nagel (2010), 27 percent of all high school students took at least one class online in 2010. This is a 14 percent increase from the previous year. The trend can be seen in middle schools as well with reports indicating as much as 21 percent of middle school students are taking some classes online (ibid). You can see, online is the place to be . . . and that is not just in Facebook but in education too!

Although some people still question the validity of online education, the number of postsecondary schools offering online classes has grown to approximately 70% (National Center for Education Statistics, n.d.). Determining the exact number is sometimes difficult because schools report online education differently, and at this time no set reporting guidelines have been established. Some schools offer entire programs online; others may offer only individual classes or some parts of a particular class online. If every school that offered some type of online component were counted, the estimated number would be close to 98%, quite an impressive statistic. The research indicates that going to school online represents the present as well as the future.

Although some potential students are still very concerned with what employers think about a degree earned online, the latest research indicates that half of all hiring managers say they would give equal consideration to both types of degrees. "In fact, many employers who are familiar with online education often like the attributes of typical online learners. These students [tend to be] independent, self-motivated, and well organized" (Carnevale, 2005). Further, according to Betts (2010) students in online programs tend to persist more than students attending on ground. We explore these qualities of successful online learners in more detail later in the book.

In the past, employers hired people with educational backgrounds to which they could relate—applicants with traditional degrees. As more and more hiring managers themselves earn degrees from online universities, expectations will change. Degrees from online institutions are becoming more the norm. The wave has started and is gaining momentum. As increasing numbers of people earn degrees from online schools, the online learner will be the employee of choice for some employers. You are on the leading edge.

So how does your online degree stack up? An online program is probably not going to be as acceptable to some as a degree from Harvard or Yale. But for those with that mindset, neither is a degree from a state on-ground school. And realistically, were you going to be able to attend Harvard or Yale anyway? We must compare apples to apples. If you obtain a degree from an online school that is accredited (see Appendix B), for all practical purposes your online degree is equivalent to a degree from a state institution or any other school in your area you opted not to attend.

THE IMPACT OF A COLLEGE DEGREE ON YOUR CAREER SUCCESS

The boss of two of the authors once said he was so proud when he finished his doctorate that the next morning he woke up, opened his door, and was ready to let all the employers in. After all, he was "Dr. Romine!" Of course, no one was at his door.

We go to school with the idea that an education will better our standard of living, which is true in most cases. But you still have to work hard and keep pursuing your goals. Most likely, you are not going to finish your degree and the next day have employers begging you to come to work, but your education can lead to greater opportunities and the ability to negotiate some job situations more easily. You will have the opportunity to change your standard of living.

Let's consider for a moment what acquiring a college education means. How does it change you, and why do you need to complete a degree program?

According to the Bureau of Labor Statistics (1999, 2004), over the next decade the upward trend of companies wanting to hire college-prepared employees will continue. As the baby boomers retire, not enough people will be available to fill these positions. Skilled, educated people will be needed to catapult the workforce forward, in areas such as management, engineering, education, and accounting, as well as many trade and technical positions.

The chart on the following page summarizes the value of a college education in terms of money and employment opportunities.

On average, a worker with a high school diploma or less will earn poverty wages. Of course, there are exceptions, but, in general, education pays. The difference in total life earnings between a high school diploma and a college degree is estimated to be $1 million (see table).

Further, a person with a college degree is less likely to be unemployed (see table). At a time when unemployment is high, it is important to note that unemployment is more than twice as high for individuals without a college education versus those with a college education.

Level of School Obtained	Weekly Earnings (in dollars)	Unemployment Rate (by percent)
Less than a high school diploma	454	14.6
High school graduates; no college	626	9.7
Some college; no degree	699	8.6
Associate's degree	761	6.8
Bachelor's degree	1,025	5.2
Master's degree	1,257	3.9
Professional degree	1,529	2.3
Doctoral degree	1,532	2.5

Data are 2009 annual averages for persons age 25 and over. Earnings are for full-time wage and salary workers.
Source: Bureau of Labor Statistics, 1999, 2004, 2011.

Moneymaking aside, though, what do you gain from a college degree? A degree obviously will give you the skills and knowledge to do your job more effectively. But in addition to that, it can give you greater self-confidence and self-esteem. A degree gives you the absolute knowledge that you were able to succeed at this endeavor—to persevere and take your education to the next level. This knowledge should give you the confidence that you can achieve anything to which you set your mind.

Finally, earning a degree is an achievement no one can ever take away from you. When one of the authors finished her degree, she told her kids, "Look what I did. Now, no matter what, I will always have this. No one can ever take an education or experience away from you." What else in your life can you say that about?

We hope we have confirmed your desire to attend school online and perhaps even made it stronger. Going to school is a privilege. It is the opportunity of a lifetime, so enjoy and embrace it. You deserve this experience! Lastly, focus on enjoying this opportunity to learn, worry less about the destination, and bask in the journey of education.

A NOTE FROM THE AUTHORS

We are extremely passionate about online education and student success and have taught, taken part in, developed, and been exposed to online education for more than 40 years collectively. We are educators who deal with online success every day. Here we share our wealth of experience to bring you inside information on how to succeed as an online student. Adopting the proven and practiced tips in this book will increase the chances of your success.

Please know that we stand behind you as you embark on becoming a successful online student. We have been there. We made it through, and so can you.

Becoming an Online Learner

Online education is where it is at. As an online student, I have control of when I learn, how I learn, and what extra I learn. I gain only as much as I put in; this is what distinguishes the online learning environment. Online education is moving toward a user driven, just-in-time model, and as an adult learner this is exactly what I want from my education.

— *Dan Record, instructional designer and online PhD student*

Power UP

⏻ Examine your motives ahead of time for wanting to take an online class/program.

⏻ Acknowledge the many myths circulating about online education. Know the difference between the myths and the facts.

⏻ Recognize that being an online student is not easier than being a student in a traditional classroom. It is just different.

⏻ Understand that time commitment, open-mindedness, autonomy, and self-motivation are expected of a successful online student.

⏻ Understand expectations for time on task: For every hour in class, students should spend 3 hours studying or reading outside of class. You will need to factor in the necessary time for your learning.

⏻ Make sure you have the necessary technical equipment and skills before you start your online class.

⏻ Understand that most endeavors are generally not smooth at the beginning. Give this one a little extra time, effort, and positive energy, and you *can* be a successful online student.

Taking on the new identity of "student" for the duration of your class or program is undeniably a *huge* undertaking. Committing to completing a degree takes deep dedication and desire. You will have to become accustomed to a brand-new mind-set. The decision to become an online student should tie heavily into your own goals and dreams because everything you are about to embark on comes down to *you*.

Because online education is still fairly new compared to traditional, in-the-classroom education, many misconceptions are still connected to it. The number one fact to remember as an online student is that this mode of education is *not* easier than being a student in a traditional classroom. It is just different.

- You have a lot more flexibility regarding time spent in and around class, but
- Online learning still takes as much if not more time compared with a traditional classroom experience.

ONLINE LEARNING: HYBRID OR ALL ONLINE

You may choose to attend one or more online courses or you may select a program that is offered entirely online. Maybe you never planned to be an online learner, but during your available time frame a required course is only offered online, making you an online learner by default. Further, many students find that schools only offer certain classes online. Whatever the situation, you will find that online courses are both similar to and different from courses in the on-ground classroom. These similarities and differences may not be what you expect, so remember to keep an open mind!

In general, university courses are categorized by modality in four ways:

1. ***On-ground, or traditional, courses.*** These are the courses that many of us grew up with. In this type of course, students go to a designated classroom at a particular time, and a teacher guides the class through the course material. Homework is assigned for the time between classes, and it is generally due from one class meeting period to the next. Some assignments, and most tests, take place during designated class time. The face-to-face (F2F) element of students and instructors meeting in real time is a major factor that distinguishes this type of course.

2. ***Online courses.*** These are courses in which the entire class is staged online. For the most part, students and instructors never meet each other in person.

3. ***Blended, or hybrid, courses.*** These courses are sometimes difficult to distinguish. A blended course has some online components and some on-ground components, but the exact mix can vary. As long as the course combines online learning and traditional classroom time in some way, it is considered blended. Most people include the idea of hybrid courses when they are talking generically about online learning. For more about blended courses, refer to Chapter 7, The Hybrid Balance.

4. ***Web-enhanced courses.*** *Web enhanced* refers to a course in which the main instruction does not take place online, but other aspects of the course do. For example, for a web-enhanced course, you retrieve your materials online. You do not actually attend class online, but your book, grade postings, and other course materials may be available online. Many schools have some type of web enhancement already, but surprisingly, some do not. Sometimes, schools begin with a web-enhanced approach before they launch a full online program.

None of these course modalities is better than the others in terms of quality. For any course, many factors make the difference in whether it is "good," including the quality of the instruction, the teacher, and the organization of the class. You will have to decide what makes a class "better" for you based on your own goals and priorities. Which of these modalities of learning sounds like it might work best for you?

What Is Expected of a Student?

To begin with, you must truly understand what you can expect to encounter in this new role as an online learner. You have the power to create your own success. Here are some of the issues that are important for an online learner to understand.

The Importance of Time Commitment

1. *You* are your own self-regulator in an online environment and to succeed you must plan and manage your time correctly.

2. Although there most likely will be a designated *day*, online courses often do not have a designated class time. You will need to determine how much time your class responsibilities will take and establish your own schedule for how to integrate coursework into your life.

3. Attending school online will take *the same if not more time* than a traditional class; what's different is how you allot the time and when you expend the time.

The Importance of Open-Mindedness

An online class is both similar to and different from a traditional classroom. Manage your expectations!

1. Have an open mind when you start online courses, and be willing to explore and become familiar with the medium. There are benefits and tricks to learning online that you will only discover if you take the time to fully explore your online course. Discover what the differences are, and learn how to take advantage of them instead of letting them intimidate you.

2. In addition to being open-minded about the style of instruction, you should be open-minded about the differences between people. Not only will the modality in which you are learning be different, but the makeup of your class may be different than what you would find at a school down the street. As you can imagine, the nature of online learning means that students in one course may come from all over the country—and all over the world.

3. Remember, only an open mind can be educated. Be willing to consider the new perspectives and new ideas that you will encounter in the course of your learning.

The Importance of Autonomy and Self-Motivation

1. Engage fully in the online environment. In an online environment, there is no need to make yourself presentable, drive to campus, locate parking, and find the classroom. But, although you may be able to participate in class while in your pajamas, you will still have to be involved in the course and commit to learning and participating.

2. Make time for class and homework. Pay attention to the workload for your courses, and plan your time appropriately. Don't let yourself be sabotaged by poor planning and procrastination. Take control of your studies.

3. You will have to do a lot of reading and writing. Be honest about the time it will take and your study skills. Commit to improving your skills.

4. Be responsive to your instructor and fellow students. Clear, timely communication matters in the online environment.

Everyone takes a different amount of time to acclimate to the online environment. It may be confusing and overwhelming at the start, but you may be surprised at how quickly you become comfortable. Give yourself a chance to adjust and get up to speed.

MYTHS AND FACTS ABOUT LEARNING ONLINE

If you are new to online learning, you may have some misconceptions or you may not be aware of some facts regarding this medium. Take a look at the table below, which lists myths and facts, and see how your own knowledge and experience with online learning measures up to reality.

Myths and Facts About Learning Online

MYTH	FACT
Online courses are less rigorous than on-ground courses.	Not necessarily. Online learning varies by course just like the traditional classroom, but, overall, you will probably be expected to do more writing, and you will need to participate more actively than you would in a traditional classroom.
Instructors in an online environment are more aloof.	It depends on the instructor, but, in many cases, online instructors are extremely responsive to student contact, and you may find it even easier to initiate contact in the online environment.
Online courses cost more than on-ground courses.	Tuition can be considerably higher, but you should also factor in expenses that online students do not have to pay for, such as gas, parking, and child care.
It is harder to interact and make friends with your classmates online.	Not necessarily. Although an online classroom is different from a traditional classroom, you may have just as much opportunity for interaction. Once you become accustomed to interacting mainly through writing, you will find plenty of opportunities to seek out others and bond with your classmates. Online courses often have a chat room or lounge area in the course where students are encouraged to go and virtually "hang out" and interact with each other. Our experience has been that students are more communicative and self-revealing in an online environment.
Online classes fit easily into a busy schedule.	Perhaps. Online courses are more flexible, but just because you do not have to go to the classroom at a certain time doesn't mean you do not need to dedicate time to your classwork.
Homework in the online environment is not the same.	Not necessarily. Actually, most of the assignments you will find online are similar to, if not the same as, those in a traditional classroom and consist of papers, exams, presentations, and so on.
Online education is lower quality.	Not so. The same accrediting bodies that work with traditional schools approve online education. Online courses frequently use the same instructors and curriculum as their traditional counterparts. The bottom line is that, just as with the traditional classroom, the online classroom is what you make of it.
Online instructors are always online and available.	Not so. Some online instructors have established office hours when they are available. Some institutions might have a 24- or 48-hour guaranteed response time. The policy varies with the instructor and the institution. It is your responsibility to find out what the policy is.
It is impossible to work in virtual teams.	Not so. Virtual teams are a reality, not only in many classroom situations but also in the workplace. A good team is a good team whether it is virtual or face to face.
There are no support systems for online learners.	Not necessarily. Online schools vary, but often they have virtual incarnations of the same resources that traditional schools have, such as labs, tutors, and libraries.

Online classrooms provide a level of interaction and give-and-take that is not always possible in a traditional classroom. Both the breadth and the depth of student engagement can be increased.

In terms of breadth, it is common for all students in the class to see each other's assignments. That can be a little hard to accept at first and you may feel intimidated, but keep in mind that the other students feel the same way.

In terms of depth, there is more time and opportunity to review the work of others as well as process your own thoughts. You will have time to really review one another's messages and assignments because these will be posted and remain in the newsgroups for the duration of the class. This differs from the need to respond immediately that is typical of face-to-face classroom discussions. Assuming it is not a scheduled discussion, an online student who needs time to process information can read the material, go for a walk while formulating a response, and then return and respond.

ARE YOU READY TO BE AN ONLINE STUDENT?

Readiness means many things. We discuss these issues in more depth later in the book, but for now, consider the following.

Time Available

You recognize you will need to schedule time for your online course. Keep in mind that for traditional students, the expectation is that for every hour in class, they will spend 3 hours studying or reading outside of class. The same formula is generally applied for online courses. A student taking a 3-credit class for 16 weeks spends about 9 hours a week out of class on assignments. It is quite possible that an online student will have a compressed class that may last for only 5 to 8 weeks. If this is the format of your online course, you will need to factor in the necessary time for learning.

Technical Equipment

Do you have access to a computer? Do you have an Internet connection? Have you satisfied the requirements of your institution regarding platform and speed of connection?

The school generally does not care what kind of computer you use. But they do have specifications for the platform you use (e.g., Windows, Mac).

1. At the very least you will need to have a word-processing application, an Internet browser, and a slide presentation application.
2. Your Internet connection speed will also need to be at a certain level. And you will want to make sure you have, or can download, certain relevant plug-ins and support programs such as Java or Adobe Acrobat.

Technical Skills

You will need to rely on your technical skills as much as your study skills in the online environment. Ask yourself these questions:

1. **Typing:** Do you know how to type? Can you type quickly and accurately?
2. **Computer Skills: How proficient are you in using a computer?** Do you know how to format a document? Do you know how to send an e-mail with an attachment?

3. **Internet and Research Skills:** How well do you leverage the Internet? Are you good at researching online?

4. **Reading:** Are you a competent reader? How fast can you read, not just from a textbook, but from a computer screen? And how well do you remember the content of what you've read?

You will find numerous resources to help you attain these skills: friends and neighbors, online tutorials, outside training courses, and maybe even training labs offered by your institution.

Your Motives

Consider why you have chosen to further your education. Ask yourself these questions:

- How serious are you?
- Why are you doing this? You might be doing it to obtain a promotion at work or to expand your career opportunities or just because you love to learn. Take time to understand fully the reason you are doing it. Own it.
- What goal will this degree help you achieve? Or is it the goal in itself? Only you can truly answer this question. Are you doing it for your own reasons or to please others?
- Do you really have the time for it?
- Do you really want to dedicate the time that will be necessary?
- Are you looking forward to what you will learn about?

Really take the time to explore your own thoughts and feelings about the details of this degree and decide whether the timing and the focus are right for you. Knowing the answer to *why* you are motivated can help you *stay* motivated.

ADAPT YOUR ATTITUDE AND PREPARE FOR SUCCESS

We said this before: Do not begin this online learning endeavor expecting it to be easy, but don't anticipate failure either. Cultivate your self-confidence and be willing to change the way you think about school and your own abilities.

Do not become distraught the minute something goes wrong. You will have assignments where you will not score as highly as you thought you would or wish you had. Everyone has those! Do not immediately think of this as failing, but try to look at it as an opportunity for improvement. Think positively: You will succeed.

The first time you do anything can be very challenging. Recall the first time you rode a bike or your first day on the job. Most new experiences are generally not smooth at the beginning, but give it time, effort, and positive energy, and you *can* be a successful online student.

Here is an analogy: Look at your introduction to online learning as you would your first visit to a foreign country. You will need time to learn the language, the lay of the land, and how to interact with the local people, but, given sufficient time and effort, it will soon become second nature. Give yourself time to adapt to online learning.

MORE POWER
TO YOU

Now is your chance to explore the topics of Chapter 1 further. For each of the chapters in this book, we have selected a few specific websites that can be helpful resources for you. Check out the sites listed here. Enjoy expanding your knowledge, and *more power to you!*

Preparing Yourself for Online Learning
www.studygs.net/online/index.htm

Is Distance Learning Right for You?
http://distancelearn.about.com/od/isitforyou/a/considering.htm

The 7 Mistakes That Distance Learners Make
http://distancelearn.about.com/od/distancelearning101/a/7mistakes.htm

For Online Students: Resources, Guides, Tips & Tutorials
www.ibritt.com/resources/stu_forstudents.htm

Note: As we all know, the Internet is dynamic and ever evolving. If any of these websites are not available or you wish to seek out additional information, we encourage you to do your own online search. Consider the concepts covered in the chapter that are most important to you, and think of various terms that could be used to describe them. For this chapter, some potential keywords include:

successful online learner

preparing online student

online readiness

When searching online, consider different ways to express ideas. Remember to use synonyms and related words. Try phrasing things in different ways. And always review more than the first few pages of the search results.

For more specific information on searching online, refer to Chapter 10.

Know Thyself: Self-Discovery for the Online Learner

2

Power UP

- Complete an honest appraisal of your skills. Ask yourself, as well as coworkers, classmates, and friends, for unbiased information on your strengths and weaknesses. Use that information to become a more well-rounded person.

- Become aware of your strengths. This allows you to identify what tasks will be easy for you and take less time.

- Become aware of your weaknesses. This allows you to identify what tasks will be more difficult for you and therefore take more time, and it also enables you to pinpoint areas where you need to improve.

- Learn how to predict how much time you need for a task. This will help you plan your study time and give others honest input in team situations regarding what you can contribute.

- Become aware of your intelligences and learning styles. Find ways to take advantage of them and use your strengths.

- Identify the peak times when you are at your best and the valley times when you are not. Try to plan your work around these times.

- Understand that personality tests are simply indicators to help you know yourself better. Think about how the results relate to being a student, specifically an online student.

n Chapter 1, we mentioned how self-analysis can be an important tool for your online education. But introspection is only one small part of the self-examination that can be helpful to you as a learner. Another important step is to look honestly at yourself and determine what comes easily for you and where you struggle, especially in terms of schoolwork and self-management.

"Know thyself," said the ancient oracle at Delphi. Knowing yourself can be helpful for everyone, but especially online learners. The better you know your own preferences, skill levels, and strengths and weaknesses, the better you will be able to adapt to and take advantage of the online environment.

WHY EXPLORE YOUR STRENGTHS AND WEAKNESSES?

Although it may not be obvious, knowing your own strengths and weaknesses does matter. It can save you time and energy. Being aware of your strengths allows you to be aware of what will be easy for you and take less time. Being able to predict how much time you need for a task will help you to plan your study time and to offer honest input regarding what you can contribute to team situations.

Your *strengths* are areas where you can mentor others who are not as skilled and help them grow.

Your *weaknesses* are areas where you will need to have patience with yourself and dedicate extra time to polishing your skills. They are also areas where you may want to look to others for help. Being aware of your weaknesses allows you to be aware of the things that will be more difficult for you and therefore take more time. If you know your weaknesses you can recognize and plan for the things that will take more time and effort for you to complete, and you can pinpoint areas where you need to try to improve.

A benefit of online education is that it allows you to be more in control of your time, so you can nurture and develop those weak areas and change them into strengths. You can also obtain feedback and help from others who are stronger than you in those areas.

You will need to be honest with team members about your skill levels. The best team assignments are produced by those teams that take advantage of all their members' skills.

Assessing yourself realistically is tough to do! Do not be afraid to ask coworkers, classmates, and friends for unbiased information on what they see as your strengths and weaknesses. You might be surprised at what you will learn, and this whole process can be an excellent opportunity for growth.

Keep in mind: Knowing your strengths and weaknesses should not lead you to depend solely on what you are good at and avoid the areas where you tend to do poorly. You will not always have the choice of focusing on your strong areas, so it is important to develop your skills in areas where you are not as strong. Your goal should be to complete an honest appraisal of your skills and then use the information to become a successful online student and a more well-rounded person. With time and perseverance, you may even develop new talents!

TOOLS FOR SELF-ASSESSMENT

We've discussed the value of asking other people for input on your strengths and weaknesses. What about other ways of assessing yourself?

A multitude of resources are available, both in print and online, that can furnish insight into your personality and preferences. Keep in mind that these tools can vary in their ease of use as well as their accuracy. Further, you will find some of the more trusted tools cost money. It will be up to you to determine whether such an investment is a smart move for you.

A clear, comprehensive self-assessment is important whether you are an online or an on-ground student. However, self-knowledge can benefit you considerably as an online student.

Personality

The personality traits you want to learn about are not those that reveal whether you laugh at jokes or like to have fun but rather those that help you understand your mind-set and attitudes when it comes to studying and learning.

Do you know your personality type? You can learn about different personality types through a web search or by reading a book on the subject. A typical search on the web using the queries *personality test* or *personality profile* will yield many free tests, and you will find numerous references to the most popular personality test, the Myers-Briggs Type Indicator (MBTI; Myers & Briggs Foundation, n.d.).

Isabel Briggs Myers and her mother developed the MBTI over 50 years ago. One of the most trusted personality assessments in the world, it is grounded in the work of psychologist C. G. Jung. This assessment evaluates your personality by looking at 16 different indicators, resulting in a scaled differentiation between sensing and intuition, thinking and feeling, introversion and extroversion, and judging and perceiving.

When taking personality assessments, remember they are simply indicators to help you know yourself better. Do not pigeonhole yourself. Rather, think about what the results mean, whether you like what they represent, and if you want to change anything. For example, you may find you are very introverted, and you would like to be more extroverted. You might create a goal of becoming more social by putting yourself in situations where you will have to interact with others. Or perhaps you like being introverted and do not wish to change. Think about how the results relate to being a student, specifically an online student.

Multiple Intelligences

Many theorists suggest that humans have multiple intelligences, which indicates that certain components of intelligence align with preferred learning styles: mathematical, visual, physical, musical, verbal, naturist, extroverted, and introverted frames of reference. You may find you are stronger in some areas than in others, and thus this would be your intelligence area. The ideas behind multiple intelligences are grounded in the theories of Howard Gardner (Gardner, 1983).

You have heard people say, "I am not that good at math." According to these theories, such individuals may not have a high mathematical intelligence. Similarly, if someone can pick up a guitar and immediately play a song, he or she would be said to have a high musical intelligence. What do you enjoy? Do you sing when the radio comes on? Do you like karaoke? Do you prefer to be outdoors hiking?

All of these preferred activities could be pointing to your intelligences. Becoming aware of your intelligences and finding ways to take advantage of them is a way to leverage your strengths.

For example, if you are a nature lover, and you like to be outside, you might find that if you were to purchase a laptop and do your work by the lake, your writing would be much easier and your thought process much more defined. This type of flexibility is yet another helpful aspect of online learning.

What about music? How can you incorporate this into studying? Think about how you learned your "ABCs." It was most likely through singing. You may find if you have musical intelligence, you want to listen to soft music while you work. Or perhaps you can put some complicated material into the lyrics of your favorite song.

The goal of self-assessment is to determine where your intelligences lie, and then consider how you can use them to be successful in an online environment. If you are interested in learning more, search on the Internet using keywords such as *multiple intelligences*, *intelligences*, and *Howard Gardner*.

Peak/Valley Times

Peak times are when you are at your best and valley times are when you are not. We believe one of the most positive factors in online learning may be just this: the ability to focus your studies during your own peak times.

Certainly there are times you are more productive throughout the day. Pay attention and figure out when those times occur. You can explore the peak/valley concept by completing an exercise and then evaluating whether it was easy for you. If you determine it was more difficult than it should have been, perhaps it was the wrong time of day. The next

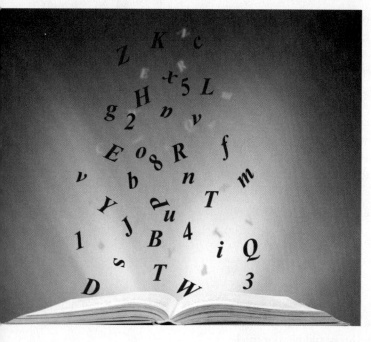

day, try another exercise at another time of day and see what happens. Were you able to complete the work more easily? It will take some time to track your patterns, but once you figure them out, you will be able to work so much more efficiently. This is another benefit of online learning. You can log in to class and study during your peak time, not your valley time.

Peak and valley times can be changeable within the day, month, or year. For example, if you are a morning person, then during the winter your peak time may be much later than in the summer.

Some people characterize peak/valley times as being a "lark" (i.e., alert and productive early in the day) or being an "owl" (i.e., more alert and productive in the evening and at night), but that description may be too simplistic. Maybe during the week, when you get up early and drink coffee, your peak times are in the morning, but on the weekend, when you sleep in, your peak times are late in the afternoon. Pay attention to these details and know what works best for you, and then capitalize on these times. That is when you will be the best learner possible and thus the most successful student. Being able to take advantage of your peak times fits right into the flexible structure of the online environment.

Ronald Gross is well known for contributing to the concept of peak and valley learning (Gross, 1999). To find more information, search on the Internet using the phrase *gross and peak learning*.

Learning Styles

The idea of learning styles relates to the way you take in and process information. Some of the most notable learning styles include visual, auditory, and tactile-kinesthetic.

- *Visual learners* learn best by seeing the teacher, concepts, diagrams, and so on. Visual learners often like to take detailed notes.

- *Auditory learners* learn best by listening. They like to talk things through and listen to others' opinions and ideas.

- *Tactile-kinesthetic learners* learn best by doing, moving, and touching. They learn via using their hands or by incorporating movement into their thinking and study.

You may want to sit back now and think about which way you learn best and then consider how this will work in an online environment. If you are a visual learner, how could you best learn online? Perhaps you could print more material and have it available to review. As an auditory learner, you might read books and messages aloud. You may even consider buying software that will change text to auditory CDs so you could listen to someone reading your book. As a tactile-kinesthetic learner, you might take ideas and map them on a piece of paper or build constructs of ideas.

Stringers and Groupers

Another learning style that relates to the way you process information is that of the stringer versus the grouper (Hill, 2001). Are you someone who likes to look only at the big picture? Do you tend to see the 40,000-foot view? Or do you like to see all of the details and work your way up?

A person who likes to look at the big picture first and then looks at the details is called a *grouper*. This type of person may begin a class by thinking about all of the assignments from a global perspective and then may consider each minute detail. Notice we say "may." Groupers sometimes don't see as many of the details as they should.

A *stringer* is a person who looks at each detail and does not see the bigger picture until the end. This type of person looks at each detail of each assignment and may not see how they all fit together. Notice we say "may." Stringers may never see the bigger picture.

Either style can take you where you want to go. And you can learn how to make your style work the best way for you. But to be a successful student, you need to be a little of both. You are going to have to stretch yourself and leave your comfort zone. If you are a grouper, you must learn to look at each detail or you may miss something of great importance. If you are a stringer, you want to look at the big picture to assure you understand how the assignments fit together. Curriculum is often constructed in such a way that the concepts build on one another. It will be helpful to you to notice and understand this structure.

It can be useful to find out the learning styles of your friends. You may find that you know several people with different styles from yours. They do say opposites attract! You can help each other along the way.

Applying Self-Assessment Information

Self-assessments can be fun and interesting, but they are most helpful if you listen to the feedback and use it to plan how you can become a more efficient and effective learner.

Remember, you do not want to pigeonhole yourself or to become frustrated with what you discover from these assessments. When you feel discouraged, realize you may be out of the comfort zone that is your learning style or your personality paradigm. Keep in mind that experiencing this discomfort can be the start of the process of learning and changing, if you choose to take advantage of it.

You will need to continue to evaluate what you can do to help enable your own success.

MORE POWER
TO YOU

Now is your chance to explore this chapter's topics further. Check out the sites listed here. Enjoy expanding your knowledge and *more power to you*!

Know Your Type
www.knowyourtype.com/google.html

Advice for Enhancing 3 Basic Learning Styles
www.sdc.uwo.ca/learning/index.html?styles

Advice on Bringing Your Learning Styles into Balance
www.mindtools.com/mnemlsty.html

Thinking and Learning Skills Course
www.ldrc.ca/projects/projects.php?id=26%20

Successful Learning: Cycle through Learning Styles
www.cdtl.nus.edu.sg/success/sl27.htm

If any of these websites are not available or you wish to seek out additional information, we encourage you to do your own online search. Consider the concepts covered in the chapter that are most important to you, and think of various terms that could be used to describe them. For this chapter, some potential keywords to search include:

> *personality profile*
> *learning styles*
> *peak learning times*

When searching online, consider different ways to express ideas. Remember to use synonyms and related words. Try phrasing things in different ways. And always review more than the first few pages of search results.

For more specific information on searching online, refer to Chapter 10.

Motivation and Goal Setting: Overcoming Obstacles

3

Power **UP**

Understand that common obstacles occur for many new online learners. Don't let these discourage you.

Plan for the cost of an online education, which may mean you have to develop a new budget and/or make some financial sacrifices.

Balance your own needs with those of others. Reassure people close to you of their importance to you even though you are focused elsewhere. Know when to put yourself first.

Acknowledge conflicting priorities (family, work, etc.) and take action. Organize your schedule, set your priorities, and be ready to revisit them occasionally.

Plan your time wisely to help you manage stress. Take it one day or one project at a time. Avoid procrastination and overcommitment.

Focus on celebrating small successes, such as the submission of your first assignment or a compliment from a classmate.

Make reasonable goals. Do your best, but admit that you do not have to be best at everything.

Follow the **SMART** model when setting a goal: **S**pecific, **M**easurable, **A**ttainable, **R**ealistic, and **T**imely.

Recognize that journaling can be an important tool for you throughout your career as a student and beyond. It can serve as a recording method, a tool for problem solving, and a stress-management strategy.

D eciding to become an online learner, or any type of student for that matter, can be very rewarding. However, there may be obstacles to overcome on the way to those rewards. Inevitably, hindrances come along with new endeavors; it is how you deal with these stumbling blocks that makes the difference. Let's take a look at some of the common challenges that new online learners often share.

FINANCIAL CONCERNS

The dreaded financial commitments that come along with enrolling in a program or a class at an institution can really put a damper on your plans. But you do have many options.

Accommodating the cost of online education may mean you have to develop a new budget and/or make some financial sacrifices. We realize everyone is in a different situation, but here is one simple example. What if you give up buying your lunch every day and brown-bag it instead? Do the calculations to see how much you could save over a year. This might help you feel better about your financial commitments.

Lunch out = $10.00
52 weeks in a year times 5 days a week = 260 days
$10.00 × 260 = a savings of $2,600 dollars a year! This will pay for one or more 3-credit classes.

Maybe you already take your lunch. If so, try analyzing where you are spending your money and think about how you might be able to pinch a penny.

- Do you smoke?
- Do you buy lottery tickets?
- Do you stop for coffee every day?
- Do you drive to the store when you could walk? With the price of gas, consider using less as much as possible. Another great feature of online classes is that you do not have to drive to class.

Further, do not forget about the financial aid and scholarships that are available (see Appendix A). The negative aspect of financial aid is that you have to pay it back, which can be quite difficult in some cases.

Statistically, many individuals graduate from college so deep in debt that even with a good-paying job, small raises make little difference because all the extra money is simply going to pay for the loans. Thus it is wise to pay for your education as you go, if at all possible. The sacrifices you make now will mean an easier time later. Also, remind yourself that eventually the debt will be cleared and you will still have the earning power of the degree. Try to be creative in looking for ways to make more money and cut expenses. You can find a way.

CONFLICTS WITH FAMILY, FRIENDS, AND SELF

Besides the worrisome financial concerns, family and friends may be envious, fearful, or negative when they hear you are going back to school or taking some online classes. Our advice is simply to give them time.

A Lack of Support

Although we all hope the people we care about in our lives will be understanding and encourage our choices, that is not always the case. Consider, though, what those around you may be feeling. People close to you may be fearful of losing you, of being left behind. Reassure them of their importance even though you are focused on other things right now. Some people may not understand your reasons for attending school online. Let them know why it matters to you, or share what you are doing in school and include them when possible. Certain individuals may be unwilling to listen to your reasons or be consoled by your words of reassurance. In these cases, you may have to make the decision to put yourself first.

You may suffer some guilt over the time you spend on school. Realize that you need to adjust your priorities for the situation, but you will not be in these circumstances forever. Remind yourself that sometimes you must put yourself first.

Spreading Yourself Too Thin

Between family and work you may have so many conflicting priorities, you are in danger of spreading yourself too thin. Beware of committing to too much at once. The best option is to organize your schedule, set your priorities, and be ready to revisit them occasionally. Be aware that you might well have to give some things up while you are pursuing your degree. But the sacrifices will be worth it. In just 2 to 4 years you can go back to your old routine but with a diploma on the wall!

You will probably feel overwhelmed sometimes. Most adults have busy, full lives before they ever add school to the equation. Just remember to take it one day or one project at a time. Do not facilitate your own stress. Recognize the need to plan your time wisely. Explore what might be easy, or sensible, for you to give up. Do your best, but admit that you cannot be perfect at everything.

Keep Your Spirits Up

You may have a hard time just envisioning that you will ever succeed at this new endeavor. But you can change this negative self-perception. If you lack confidence, focus on celebrating small successes: the submission of your first assignment or a compliment from a classmate or instructor. Use a journal to track your incremental improvements and successes.

Be sure not to set yourself up for failure. Make reasonable goals, do not procrastinate, manage your stress, and beware of taking too many classes at once. If you are haunted by the past, you have to move beyond it. For instance, if you dropped out of school or failed a course before, give yourself permission to try again now. Do your best to live in the present.

The all-star basketball player Michael Jordan once said, "I missed 100% of the shots I never took." This is a new situation, and you are different. Give yourself a chance to change and grow.

REACHING GOALS MEANS SETTING GOALS

The most successful people are those who set goals—for their career, for their self-development, and for their personal life. A manageable way to set goals is to first set your goals for the next 3 years or more and then to break these goals into smaller chunks.

Studies show that articulating significant goals leads to an increase in a person's effort and thus success (Hamner & Harnett, 1974; Locke, 1968). Further, this success leads to higher self-esteem, which contributes to future success!

Setting goals is critical, and here are some questions to consider: First, why are you setting a goal? Is your goal a personal one, a performance goal for the course, or a long-term goal, such as completing your degree?

Think about a day when you woke up and had no idea of what you wanted to accomplish. Did you accomplish anything? More often than not, the answer to that question is no. Explore what you want: is it earning an A, reaching for a better work/life balance, or just improving your participation in class? Then divide each goal into smaller, more immediately manageable parts and plan how you will attain each one. You may feel more comfortable setting mostly short-term goals or you may prefer to take the long view, but whatever you do, have goals.

Have you ever ended a day after completing all your goals and felt fantastic and invigorated? If the answer is yes, it is probably because you accomplished your goals and you felt successful.

Steps in Goal Setting

When setting a goal, follow the **SMART** model: **S**pecific, **M**easurable, **A**ttainable, **R**ealistic, and **T**imely. For example, you had set the goal of *acquiring an education* or you would not be in school.

Let's apply the **SMART** model to that goal:

Goal:	Acquire an education
Specific:	Gain an associate's degree within 2 years of beginning a program
Measurable:	Measure by assessing whether the degree is complete within 2 years
Attainable:	Do you have the resources in place to pursue this goal?
Realistic:	Is this a realistic goal at this time in your life, given what you have going on?
Timely:	Two years is normally what would be required to complete an associate's degree, so this is a realistic time frame.

The preceding list outlined a long-term goal. Now break the goal into smaller parts:

Goal:	Finish 30 credits my first year (you fill in the following sections)
Specific:	
Measurable:	
Attainable:	
Realistic:	
Timely:	

Now let's break the goal into smaller sections:

Goal:	Finish my first class within 3 months
Specific:	
Measurable:	
Attainable:	
Realistic:	
Timely:	

Finally, *even more* specifically:

Goal:	Finish my first class within 3 months with a grade of no less than a B
Specific:	
Measurable:	
Attainable:	
Realistic:	
Timely:	

Here's the bottom line: You know how you eat an elephant: one bite at a time. Set your goals, determine the reasons for them, and then establish manageable subgoals.

When each of us started our academic programs, we had no idea if we could complete them. But we were motivated and we set goals. Each of us decided we would complete one class at a time. And here we are, finished with the programs.

For more information on setting goals, do an online search for *SMART* and *goal setting*. Many wonderful resources are available to you. There are also additional goal worksheets found at the back of the book.

JOURNALING AS A TOOL FOR SUCCESS

Journaling has a long history. People from generations ago recorded their experiences and thoughts over time. Archived journals have made it possible for us to tap into the experiences of others and learn firsthand about the past. The literature is convincing about the many advantages of journaling as a personal strategy for success (Baikie & Wilhelm, 2005) as well as an educational strategy for success (Kerka, 1996). Many schools have even made journaling a requirement of the curriculum.

Journaling can be an important tool for you throughout your career as a student and beyond. Remember, there is no right or wrong way to journal, no particular format or style.

Although many people associate a pen and paper with journaling, you can record your voice on a tape recorder as your journal or type a document on your computer. Find the method that is most comfortable for you. The more at ease you feel with the way you have chosen to journal, the simpler it will be to express your thoughts, feelings, and opinions freely.

We do recommend some type of system where thoughts are recorded somewhere tangibly. Thinking is essential, of course, but exporting these thoughts to another format constitutes true journaling.

Reasons for Journaling

Journaling can be constructive in numerous ways.

1. *A method of recording your experiences for later reference.*   As you continue your online education, journaling can help you remember the highlights of your student experiences, so you can go back and reread them for motivation and encouragement.

   You can track what you did that worked best for you in your classes, so you can use those strategies again. Document what did not work out well for you too, so you can learn from those experiences and avoid them.

2. *A tool for problem solving.*   You can use journaling as a strategy to problem-solve. You can explore your concerns regarding school by journaling, so you can become aware of, and possibly overcome, those obstacles.

3. *A stress-management strategy.*   Lastly, journaling is an excellent tool for managing stress. Studies show that taking the time to express your thoughts and feelings in a journal not only makes it easier to process things that happen, but it also helps people deal more effectively with stressful situations.

So use journaling as a method to learn from your experiences and explore your thoughts, rather than merely as a way to track the bad things that happen to you or to express negative thoughts. Writing with a focused goal in mind will be more beneficial than just random jottings.

Another part of the whole concept of journaling is self-reflection. You may like to exercise and think, or drive and think, or ride a horse and think. In a sense, reflection is part of the journaling process, but you have to take it one step further and solidify these thoughts surging in your mind into a permanent format. One of the authors of this book thinks things through while on her morning run. As her endorphins flow, her mind gets going. When she returns home, she quickly journals the ideas, thoughts, and revelations she had while she was jogging.

Simply put, journaling is a powerful tool that can help you take concepts, thoughts, and ideas and make them more tangible and thus more useful to you. Journaling is a great technique simply to learn more about yourself. It is one of the best ways to fully explore your new identity as a student, uncover the reasons you became a student, learn about your motivators as a student, and become a more effective student.

For more in-depth information on types of journals and how journaling can help everyone from chronic pain sufferers to adult students, do an Internet search with the phrase *benefits journaling*, and peruse the results.

Freewriting

Freewriting is a form of journaling. There are many ways and reasons to freewrite; here we focus on freewriting as a way to relieve stress, encourage relaxation in your life, and find inspiration.

To use freewriting to help yourself de-stress, visualize a place that makes you feel relaxed. It can be anywhere. Paint a vivid picture in your mind of how this soothing place looks, smells, and sounds. Come back to this same place each time you freewrite. Once you have yourself in your tranquil place, begin to write, type, or draw anything that comes into your mind. Your writing does not have to be a complete sentence or picture. Grammar rules need not apply. Jot down anything that pops into your head, even if it is the phrase, "I cannot think of what to write." When something new comes into your head, record it. Do not worry about the continuity of your thoughts. Just write, type, or draw. If your writing is too neat and coherent, you probably have not loosened up enough.

Freewriting relieves stress because it helps rid your mind of clutter. Many of the random thoughts that continually bombard you can be recorded during freewriting and unchained from your subconscious. Freewriting should not be forced. Use it to soothe and calm your mind whenever you need it. You will find a sample of a freewriting exercise used to relieve stress and anxiety below.

> Butterflies around the corner. Life is an adventure. Rabbits. Cotton candy and daffodils. Never ending Mist free. Penguins gliding on cherry Ice, incredible feelings and not sure what to say, rainbow, lasting impressions, Helmet, life lessons and papers stacked up, obtaining things done in time, clock wrench, paper dolls, books, what to say next. Harper, what am I doing? What is next? Vivid yellow lucid dreams and a summer breeze drifting with monumental moments— Fear, along with excitement!

Freewriting is also an excellent way to find inspiration for problematic assignments. For example, you may have been given a writing assignment you do not quite understand. A beginning step is just to process the information. Begin with a blank sheet of paper or computer screen and then just start writing or typing your thoughts around the subject. Next, do research, and as new ideas come to you, type or write them into the document. If you continue this practice, sooner or later you may have some great ideas available you can use to formulate your paper.

MORE POWER
TO YOU

Now is your chance to explore this chapter's topics further. Check out the sites listed here. Enjoy expanding your knowledge and *more power to you!*

Goal Setting for Everyone
www.mygoals.com/

Study Guides and Strategies (Learning)
www.studygs.net/

Journaling for Stress Management
http://stress.about.com/od/generaltechniques/p/profilejournal.htm

Freewriting
www.delmar.edu/engl/instruct/stomlin/1301int/lessons/process/freewrit.htm

Motivating Yourself
www.studygs.net/motivation/

If any of these websites are not available or you wish to seek out additional information, we encourage you to do your own online search. Consider the concepts covered in the chapter that are most important to you, and think of various terms that could be used to describe them. For this chapter, some potential keywords to search include:

> *staying motivated*
>
> *setting academic goals*
>
> *planning personal budget*

When searching online, consider different ways to express ideas. Remember to use synonyms and related words. Try phrasing things in different ways. And always review more than the first few pages of search results.

For more specific information on searching online, refer to Chapter 10.

The Commitments of an Online Student: Managing Your Priorities

4

Power UP

- Make more time by using your available time wisely.

- Apply time-management techniques such as using a personal calendar, addressing all of your responsibilities, and saying *no*.

- Avoid procrastination. Plan ahead, and be aware of how much time it will take to do something. Don't wait until the last minute.

- Know when to ask for help. Realize that sometimes the best option is to reach out to others.

- Recognize the relationship between stress management and time management. Successfully managing one will help with managing the other.

- Take responsibility for your own stress level. Recognize your stressors and how you respond, and be aware of the best ways for you to manage stress.

- Surround yourself with supportive people.

- Treat yourself as a priority.

Power UP

At this point in your life, you probably have plenty to keep you busy and active: your family, job, friends, and hobbies. Being an online student will just add one more ingredient to that complicated mix. In the interest of being successful throughout your life, not just at your job or in school, we invite you to explore two concepts: time management and stress management. Having an understanding of both will make it much easier to meet all your commitments and stay sane while doing it!

Time management is a common term, but what does it actually mean? For our purposes, time management means:

- Knowing how much time you have.

- Knowing how much time it takes to complete different tasks.

- Knowing how to manipulate circumstances to fit your obligations into the time you have.

Overall, it means making *more* time by using the time you have wisely. You can adjust your schedule in different ways. For instance, you can use time in waiting rooms and while commuting. You can get up earlier or go to bed later.

Procrastination is another common term, but it means more than just waiting until the last minute. It also implies not planning ahead and not recognizing how much time it will take to do something. Do not wait until Saturday to start a paper due Monday. If you have a question but your instructor does not have weekend office hours, you will be stuck! Time management and procrastination are not just relevant to school. They can impact all aspects of your life. To be efficient and effective in anything you do, *avoid procrastination and practice good time management.*

The tendency to procrastinate is magnified even more in an online environment because you do not have to go to class and run the risk of being humiliated if your work is not done. You can just not submit a paper and, although your faculty member may contact you, no one else will know. This situation can also occur when it comes to participation. If you delay participating, no one may notice but you and your instructor. But, imagine a snowball rolling downhill. It becomes bigger and more out of control the further downhill it goes. So avoid procrastination and set yourself up for success.

AVOIDING PROCRASTINATION

How to avoid procrastination is fairly simple to summarize but a bit harder to actually do. Here are some steps to take:

- Plan ahead.
- Be aware of how you are actually spending your time.
- Recognize how long things take to complete in real time.
- Do not put off obligations until the last minute.

Procrastination is about time management, but it is also about fairness. Be fair to yourself and those around you by planning skillfully. Be fair to your assignments and your classmates by giving projects the time they deserve. Don't be satisfied with rushing through assignments at the last minute just because you usually earn a barely passing grade. Part of doing the best you can is not procrastinating.

Knowing your strengths and weaknesses can also be constructive in fighting procrastination. You may want to review the section on Personality in Chapter 2 now, with an eye toward how your preferences, strengths, and weaknesses affect the way you plan your time.

Ahead we also discuss time management and stress management. Procrastination contributes negatively to both. If you procrastinate, you are not managing your time well—and you are probably increasing your level of stress.

MANAGING YOUR TIME SUCCESSFULLY

Time management is complex because there are many considerations and no specific formula exists. Everyone has to evaluate his or her personal situation and abilities and figure out what works best.

Answering All of Your Responsibilities

Most everyone today has to juggle commitments. Ideally, you can make a single schedule for how your day or week or month will go and stick to it, but, in reality, new commitments arise and events are cancelled or reprioritized. The picture is constantly changing.

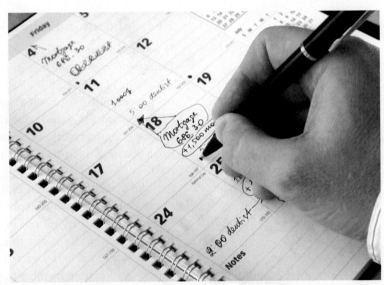

Not everything is within your control, which can make it difficult to stick to your initial plan. So you will need to constantly prioritize and reprioritize to adapt to the changing nature of your obligations over time. For instance, if you have a big work project due one week, you should anticipate not having as much time to devote to school during that period. You will also need to take responsibility for your decisions when juggling commitments.

Using a Personal Calendar

Creating your own personalized calendar can be a helpful tool for tracking and managing your responsibilities and showing you how your personal, professional, and school life overlap. A successful person usually has one calendar that shows *all* of his or her obligations and plans. This technique can enable you to manage your life much more effectively. You can use a day planner, a wall or desk calendar, Microsoft Outlook, your smartphone, or whatever works for you. The important thing is not *how* you track the demands on your time but that you *do* track them.

To find more information and tools on time management, do a Web search on *time management* and *time management tools*. There is also a time log at the back of the book that you can use to track and analyze your time.

Saying No

People often have a problem saying *no* to others, but it is OK to say no gracefully and for a good reason. No one wins when you accept a responsibility you know you cannot fulfill or when you realize you will not be able to meet an obligation but you do not speak up. Saying *no* is not about being cruel, unresponsive, or a slacker; rather it is about being honest and effective. Now that you are in school, the need to say *no* may arise more frequently than before because you have more commitments.

When It Is Necessary

When you are beginning to feel out of control or overwhelmed or when you *know* you will not be able to perform a task, it may be time to consider saying *no*. Be realistic about your abilities and your obligations! Tune in to your own feelings and be aware of your commitments, as well as your stress level, and try to judge your capabilities fairly.

Realize that sometimes, even when you might want to say *no*, it is just not possible. Distinguish between those times when it is a viable option and when it is not.

How to Say It

Saying *no* is not about making excuses, throwing fits, or avoiding guilt. Do not beat around the bush. Say *no* gracefully and succinctly. Do not list all the reasons for your refusal. Be brief, reasonable, and calm, and realize your refusal will not make the world crumble. Be direct and apologetic. If you can suggest alternative solutions that might help the situation, that's even better. Do your best to make the situation as painless as possible for those affected by your actions.

Be Confident in Deciding to Say *No*

If you determine that saying *no* is justified, do not second-guess yourself. Own your *no*! Don't agonize over whether it was the right decision after it is done. Your refusal to do something might not be painless, but it should free you to address other, more important obligations with a clear mind and clear conscience. It is easier to make decisions and move forward if you are honest about what you can and cannot do. Saying *no* is not about getting you off the hook or shirking responsibility. The goal in being honest about when you need to say *no* is to help improve efficiency and to avoid letting yourself or others down.

Like so many of the concepts discussed in this book, knowing when and how to say *no* can benefit you as much out of school as in class. With regard to the online classroom, knowing when to say *no* can be an essential skill for working in project teams. For instance, if you will be unable to complete part of a team project, you should speak up as soon as you realize it, so the team can make other arrangements. Perhaps you can trade with another team member to work on a part that is due later.

Conversely, outside the classroom, if you have overscheduled yourself and you find you must cancel lunch with a friend in order to complete an assignment, tell the person as soon as you realize it. Be forthright and apologetic, but honest. Try to reschedule for a more suitable time. If money is an issue, perhaps you can offer to cook dinner. If you can come up with an attractive trade-off for those you would otherwise be letting down, then do so.

The Frequency of Saying *No*

Knowing when and how to say *no* is key, and it is also important to recognize how often you are making refusals. If you find yourself doing it a lot, there is a bigger problem. Step back and take stock of what is going on. Are you overscheduling yourself? Are you being unrealistic about how long tasks really take to complete? Are you procrastinating? Are you a people pleaser who says *yes* to everything and then realizes you cannot possibly do it all? Be honest. You can save yourself a lot of trouble by saying *no* at the beginning, rather than saying *yes* and then changing your mind.

Look at your schedule and consider your true feelings about your obligations. It is acceptable to back out of a commitment or opt to say *no* occasionally for a good reason, but if you are making a habit of not meeting your commitments, watch out! Respect others and yourself by being realistic and honest about your responsibilities and capabilities.

ASKING FOR HELP

Sometimes the online environment can be confusing. Instructors don't always consider what it is like to be a student, and so they may not always supply the right information or adequate instructions to guide you through assigned tasks. Or maybe you just need more details on what is expected. Asking for help can often move you past a hurdle, so you can continue to accomplish all the goals on your learning path. Asking for help has much in common with saying *no*. You need to consider the following factors.

When It Is Appropriate

Of course, you never want to abuse help by asking for it all the time without trying to think a challenge through on your own first. But if you have struggled with the problem and repeatedly hit a wall, it is time to ask for someone else's input or guidance.

You also want to make sure you do not wait until the last minute to ask for help because other people have tight schedules too. You do not know how long it will take someone to respond to your request, so poor planning ahead of time may really put you behind. This is another reason it is always wise to avoid procrastination and start on your assignments right away. Then if you run up against any roadblocks and need to ask for help, there will be adequate time.

Make the Request the Right Way

As with saying *no*, be polite but also detailed and direct. Ask nicely and let the other person know you have tried to figure it out on your own first. If someone is going to help you, he or she needs to know exactly where you are stuck and what solutions you have already tried.

Also remember that asking for help is often reciprocal. Consider people studying together. It is often at the request of one person who needs help understanding course concepts, but when two people study together they usually both end up with a clearer understanding of the subject matter. If you ask someone for help, it can often mean you may be *giving* help to that person some other time.

Be Comfortable Asking

The largest mistake people make is equating asking for help with weakness. Your commitment to education is a huge obligation, and you are working hard. Sometimes you have exhausted all avenues and the best option is to reach out for some help. So equate being able to request help in appropriate situations with strength.

Analyze Your Requests for Help

Like saying *no*, monitor how often and why you ask for help. Why do you need help? Did you do all the reading and follow all directions before you asked for help, or are you just looking to others to get you through the hard parts? Learn to rely on yourself and try diverse approaches to solving problems. Are you totally lost in the class? Make sure you enroll in courses that are appropriate for your learning level rather than trying to skip out of lower-level courses. Are there certain subjects where you always have trouble and know you will need help? You might want to let your instructor know beforehand, so he or she can suggest any relevant resources or supports that the school provides.

STRESS MANAGEMENT

Some stress can be productive. It motivates you and makes you sharp. Stress only becomes a problem when it starts impacting your performance negatively.

How is stress management related to time management? Successfully managing your time can help you eliminate stress, and successfully managing your stress can aid you in the effective use of your time. Just as there are lots of methods for managing time, many strategies for managing stress are available too.

We have already mentioned that journaling can be a great reliever of stress. Here are some additional ideas to keep in mind regarding stress management.

Taking Responsibility

Many times we are powerless over the factors that cause stress in our lives, of course, but how we respond to them *is* completely in our control. These three steps will help you take responsibility for your stress:

1. *Recognize* **what** *stresses you out.* Rush-hour traffic? Having too many commitments at the same time? A screaming child? People who do not listen? Computer problems? There are too many potential stressors in the world to list here. But it would behoove you to pay attention and determine your so-called hot buttons. Just knowing them sometimes decreases their ability to affect you.

2. *Recognize* **how** *you respond.* What happens when you are stressed? Do you become short-tempered? Tired? Depressed? Do you react similarly to all stressors or differently every time? Know how stress affects you so you can prepare yourself and respond appropriately.

3. *Be aware of the best ways for* **you** *to manage stress.* What relaxes you? How do you take your mind off your troubles? Exercise, hobbies, spending time alone, journaling, spending time with family/friends, talking it out? Know what helps you release stress. Experiment with new ways occasionally; you might find it helpful to have a variety of methods at your disposal. Know how to fit those therapeutic activities into your schedule. And do it before your stress levels reach the point of desperation!

Surrounding Yourself with Supportive People

Accepting the support of people around you, whether they are friends, relatives, or classmates, can help you deal with negative experiences. Supportive people can remind you to keep in perspective whatever is bothering you. If you do not already have a strong social network of friends and family, never fear. Interactions in the online classroom can result in friendships that will last a lifetime. Your classmates are some of your best resources. They can support and commiserate with you, and they know what you are going through like no one else does.

Treating Yourself as a Priority

Part of managing your stress is taking time for yourself so you will be better able to meet your responsibilities. In today's busy world, it is easy to devote every spare moment to work, school, family, and friends. But remember that making yourself a priority can benefit all those other activities as well by helping you become a more relaxed, focused, and productive person.

If you have difficulty finding personal time, review the previous section on saying *no*. Remember, if you are in a positive state of mind, you are more likely to be productive as well as receptive to learning.

MORE POWER
TO YOU

Now is your chance to explore this chapter's topics further. Check out the sites listed here. Enjoy expanding your knowledge and *more power to you*!

Developing a Schedule
www.studygs.net/schedule/

Avoiding Procrastination
www.studygs.net/attmot3.htm

Home–Work Life Balance
www.organizedassistant.com/article/Article/
Reclaiming-Self—Making-Time-For-Yourself/66

Learning to Say *No* and Mean It
www.confidenceworld.com/members2/work7.htm

If any of these websites are not available or you wish to seek out additional information, we encourage you to do your own online search. Consider the concepts covered in the chapter that are most important to you, and think of various terms that could be used to describe them. For this chapter, some potential keywords to search include:

> *avoid procrastination*
>
> *time management*
>
> *stress management*

When searching online, consider different ways to express ideas. Remember to use synonyms and related words. Try phrasing things in different ways. And always review more than the first few pages of search results.

For more specific information on searching online, refer to Chapter 10.

The Online Classroom and Community

5

Know your instructor is the subject-matter expert. Contact your instructor for issues directly related to the specific class.

Recognize that online learning can mean exposure to a wide range of people from all over the world, from every age group, gender, and background. You can potentially learn as much from your classmates as you do from the instructor.

Recognize that it is worthwhile to read other people's postings. It will enable you to learn what their personalities are like and what you might have in common.

Know what venue is appropriate for various types of communication in your classroom.

Acknowledge that you will probably be assigned to project teams quite often during the course of your online education.

Initiate contact with your team members and clarify roles, responsibilities, and expectations right away.

Understand you should contact your advisor for any concerns relevant to your program, schedule, or a faculty member.

Identify the role and contact information for the tech support department, and understand you should contact tech support only for specific problems involving the online system of the course.

Take the time to explore your institution's website, or virtual campus, and see what it offers.

When we say the "online classroom and community," who exactly are we talking about? The foremost members of your online classroom are obvious: you, your fellow classmates, and your instructor. In some cases there may also be a teaching assistant or other types of specialized positions such as peer tutors or course assistants. The members of your online classroom include anyone who is in your first line of contact for the course.

What exactly your online community is may be a bit hazier. The members of this community can include all those individuals just mentioned in addition to the dedicated resources available from your school but outside your classroom. People such as advisors, program chairs, and librarians, as well as individuals and groups from the wide world of the Internet can be resources for you.

For each of these groups, let's look at who they are, what you might expect from them, and when it is appropriate to contact them.

YOUR INSTRUCTOR

Instructor, teacher, professor, facilitator—whatever term is used to identify him or her, this person is the subject-matter expert who will lead you through the course material and give you direction regarding what is expected and what resources are available to you.

Know who in your online community to contact for specific concerns.

Depending on the requirements of the school, your instructor probably has at least a master's degree in a subject relevant to the teaching topic, if not a PhD or other type of doctorate/terminal degree (EdD, DBA, DM, JD). In the online environment, instructors generally post a brief biography as well as virtual office hours when they are available for communication and their specific course policies. Information about instructor availability and other resources should be clearly stated. You will need to explore your online classroom thoroughly. Do not be afraid to ask questions prior to enrolling in an institution, and if you do not like the answers, consider looking for another school.

Beware of coming to your online classroom with the expectation that the instructor's role will mirror what you have experienced in other classrooms, online or on-ground. Instructor roles can vary quite a lot in the online environment, by individual instructor as well as by institution. Some instructors see themselves more as guides and mentors and are willing to converse with you at length. Others are only available to students for specific, limited concerns, and depending on the school, there may be other people whose role it is to respond to your questions or problems, such as learning assistants, preceptors, or course coordinators.

When to Contact Your Instructor

Communication with your instructor depends on the boundaries he or she sets. In general, it is safe to assume that unless otherwise stated, you can contact your instructor for any of your questions regarding the course content, assignments, and activities. Whenever you do not understand a concept in the reading or discussion, or expectations are not clear regarding assignments, grading standards, or due dates, do not hesitate to contact your instructor. If you are having a problem on your project team or having personal problems that affect your class performance, contact your instructor as soon as possible to minimize misunderstandings.

For course scheduling, graduation requirements, or computer problems, your instructor is *not* the appropriate resource. Who is depends on how the school organizes its online academic and administrative departments. You might be able to ask your instructor where you can turn in these situations, but do not expect the instructor to address them.

You are responsible for exploring those other resources, and it's a good idea to find out about them ahead of time, so you are not caught in a bind. While you are exploring the online class, put together a course contact list and keep it close at hand.

Response Time

How quickly should you expect your instructors to respond to your questions? It can vary per institution, but find out by asking them what to expect or by posting an actual question. Some instructors adhere very strictly to their scheduled office hours; others are more flexible. Some respond immediately to every message, whereas others may take hours or even days to get in touch with you. Be willing to follow up; never be satisfied with not receiving a response. If your instructor does not respond or does not show up to class, contact an advisor or administrator at the school and apprise them of the situation.

Finally, know what venue is appropriate for various types of communication in your classroom. Many instructors have a space in the online course specifically for posting questions about the class, so all students will see their answers. If your classroom does not have such a space, e-mail may be the most viable option. Explore your online classroom to figure it out.

Do not ask about grades in a public forum. It is a good idea to track your grades and know where you stand throughout your academic career. However, in a classroom, you would not want to raise your hand and question the instructor about your grade in front of the entire class. So don't do that in your online class. Contact your instructor directly through e-mail or by phone to discuss any grading concerns that you may have.

YOUR CLASSMATES

Your classmates are an obvious and easy resource for you to consult. Do not be afraid to lean on them for support.

When you have a question you believe is too foolish or obvious to pose to your instructor, or if you just need minor clarification, or even if you are just curious to know what others think, turning to your fellow students is the simple solution. And if you need someone to commiserate with you over the difficulty of an assignment, no one is more appropriate than one of your classmates. You may end up learning almost as much from your classmates as you do from your instructor. Your classmates come from different backgrounds and can provide a wealth of resources and knowledge. Their varying perspectives and learning styles can give you insight into the course content that you might not otherwise discover.

Do not be intimidated by the variety of people in your classes; online learning can mean a wide range of people from all over the world share your classroom. Engaging with your classmates can lead to lifelong friendships.

Read other people's postings to become acquainted with their personalities and see what you might have in common. You will probably be able to tell from the way people introduce themselves and respond to the discussion questions who will be the best ones to ask particular questions. You will discover who is serious and knowledgeable, who is more lighthearted and relaxed. What type of question you have or interaction you are looking for will determine which one of your classmates you wish to engage. There also may be times when you want to pose a query to the entire class to gain a wide variety of answers.

The rules and regulations for contacting your fellow students are in no way as structured and definite as those for other parties in the online community, so do talk to your classmates when you feel the urge. Of more concern is the *where/how* of the communication. Do not start personal conversations in class areas dedicated to specific tasks or questions. Usually there will be a lounge or other chat area set aside in the online classroom where students can communicate more casually with one another. E-mail is always an option too.

YOUR PROJECT TEAMS

Because project teams are a subset of your classmates, the same information just described applies to them, just within a narrower scope. Project teams are typically formed to address larger assignments, so students can share expertise and abilities, support each other in their learning, and produce synergy through the collaboration. Some research suggests that, depending on the individual and the group situation, people may learn more when

they work in groups (Rowland, Lederhouse, & Satterfield, 2004). They learn more about the subject matter and gain team skills as well. Virtual teams are also commonplace in the working world, so working in this way in the classroom will help you be effective under similar circumstances at your job. You will probably be assigned to project teams quite often during the course of your online education.

The question that always arises regarding project teams is "How is it possible to work in teams online?" But there is every reason for it to work! You have classmates who are your potential team members. You have virtual meeting rooms. You have many ways in which to dialogue, such as chat rooms, Instant Messenger, and e-mail. You are offered even more flexibility to meet with your team than in a face-to-face environment. All of these options make team interaction not only possible but equally as productive as it is in the on-ground environment.

Project teams are usually created by breaking a class into several subgroups. The number of people on a team may vary. Sometimes an instructor takes care to ensure that teams include members of differing experience or expertise or that members are in close time zones to facilitate working together. You will be responsible for helping your team run smoothly and succeed.

If you are on a project team, a percentage of your grade will be based on the team's work, and sometimes that may be significant. You may be graded on a project as a whole, and sometimes team members grade one another anonymously on their group participation. So be proactive whenever you are assigned to a team. Take the following steps:

1. Initiate contact with your team members as soon as they are identified.

2. Make sure you all have a common understanding of the requirements for the project.

3. Start clarifying individual roles, responsibilities, and expectations right away.

4. Set up a timeline for achieving the project milestones that allows you to progress reasonably toward the final due date.

Communication is key for virtual teamwork. We will say it again: Be sure to contact your team members as soon as you are grouped together, and keep up communication throughout the project. Because you have a designated reason to be in contact with them, and you have built rapport, often team members can be great resources for other questions you have about the course. As with the rest of your education, the difference between a successful team experience and a miserable one is often in the planning and preparation. Be sure to spend adequate time early on to clarify roles and expectations.

YOUR ADVISOR

Your instructor is there to help you with issues relevant to the course, and your classmates can provide personal support. However, your advisor is the one to consult for questions on scheduling classes, financial aid, or issues with a faculty member.

Do not ask your instructor about your next start date, and do not ask your advisor how to gain extra credit. Determine whose job it is to address which specific concerns (in the case of the example noted here, the answers are the opposites). You will gather answers more easily, and the various people who are your resources will thank you for not wasting their time. Because your advisor is a resource outside the classroom, you will ordinarily communicate by e-mail.

TECH SUPPORT

Tech support is the general term for the department of people dedicated to keeping the computer systems for the school up and running smoothly. You will most likely communicate with tech support personnel by e-mail or phone.

Take note of the telephone number for tech support and their hours of operation. Not all schools have technical experts available 24/7, so find out exactly when you can contact them. You might find it helpful to know their busiest times (e.g., Sunday afternoons, before classes start up on a Monday). Service will probably be delayed during those periods.

Recognize when it is appropriate to contact tech support and when it is not. Call tech support if you cannot access your course, if links or buttons in your course are not functioning, or if there seem to be technical problems with the course system.

Tech support is generally *not* there to help you format a document, understand a software application, or solve your hard drive problems. In most cases, tech support should never be used as an excuse for why you didn't submit an assignment. If downtimes are scheduled for certain systems, students are generally informed ahead of time, and you will be expected to take that into consideration and work around it.

OTHER SCHOOL RESOURCES

Just as you would explore the traditional campus of your school if you were there, take the time to check out your institution's website, or virtual campus, and see what it offers. Here are some initial areas to investigate:

- Does the school have an online bookstore? If so, what are the policies regarding ordering and shipping books? If not, where should you acquire course materials?

- What kind of learning support is available? Are there tutorials, learning labs, or a writing center? Are live tutors available for any subject?

- Is there a school library? How do you access it, and what type of assets and aid does it offer?

An online institution often has numerous other virtual resources. Take the time to explore your school and the resources available for each course you take.

MORE POWER
TO YOU

Now is your chance to explore this chapter's topics further. Check out the sites listed here. Enjoy expanding your knowledge and *more power to you*!

Instructional Strategies for Online Courses
www.ion.uillinois.edu/resources/tutorials/pedagogy/instructionalstrategies.asp

Tools, Tips, and Software Online
www.librarysupportstaff.com/ed4you.html#usetools

Adults Returning to School
www.collegeinfo.org/adults.pdf

Six Ways to Work More Effectively with a Virtual Team
www.microsoft.com/atwork/worktogether/virtual.mspx

Cooperative Learning
www.studygs.net/coolearn.htm

If any of these websites are not available or you wish to seek out additional information, we encourage you to do your own online search. Consider the concepts covered in the chapter that are most important to you, and think of various terms that could be used to describe them. For this chapter, some potential keywords to search include:

> *virtual work teams*
> *building successful teams*

When searching online, consider different ways to express ideas. Remember to use synonyms and related words. Try phrasing things in different ways. And always review more than the first few pages of search results.

For more specific information on searching online, refer to Chapter 10.

Navigating Learning Management Systems

Power UP

- Know that the acronym *LMS* (learning management systems) refers to software programs that organize and provide access to online learning services for students, teachers, and administrators.

- Recognize that most LMSs share many of the same elements, although they may be organized differently.

- Understand that your school may have its own proprietary LMS specifically designed for the faculty and students at your institution.

- Identify the common areas of all online classrooms.

- Take the time to explore and navigate your school's LMS before your class starts.

- Be aware that regardless of LMS, whether or not a final proctored exam is required depends on the school offering the course. Always check before you start a course to see if a proctored exam is required and, if so, where it will be administered.

All the content created for you as an online student has to be stored and delivered. *Learning management systems* (*LMSs*) are software programs that organize and provide access to online learning services for students, teachers, and administrators. Typically, an LMS provides an instructor or other school agent with a way to create and deliver content, monitor student participation, and track student performance. An LMS may also give students the ability to use interactive features such as threaded discussions, videoconferencing, and discussion forums. Although LMSs differ in presentation and programming, the Advanced Distance Learning Group, sponsored by the U.S. Department of Defense, has created a set of specifications called Shareable Content Object Reference Model (SCORM) to encourage the standardization of learning management systems (www.bytepile.com/definitions-l .php). As a result, many of the mainstream LMSs for the postsecondary (college) market are SCORM compliant.

Some institutions create their own proprietary LMSs, but most take advantage of the range of products on the market. The most common LMSs that universities and colleges use today are Moodle, LearningStudio^SM, and Blackboard. Your school's LMS is probably one of these.

This chapter describes the most common LMSs and offers some tips on using them successfully. Even if your school uses a system other than those mentioned here, or has created its own LMS, many of the same organizational principles and properties still apply.

WHAT TO EXPECT IN YOUR ONLINE CLASSROOM

Regardless of the LMS used, the online classroom usually contains the following basic areas:

- Classroom announcements
- Academic discussion, where discussion questions are posted
- Course content, including instructional materials and information
- Assignments and assessments
- A chat room, lounge, or other virtual location for socializing with classmates
- Resources related to the course content, such as web links and articles

When you take a course using any of the LMSs mentioned, you might be asked to view multimedia material, such as videos, animations, or simulations. So before you start, check with your school and/or instructor to find out what software to install on your computer. Examples of this software may include, but are not limited to, the following:

- Adobe Reader (free download at http://get.adobe.com/reader/)
- Adobe Flash Player (free download at www.adobe.com/go/getflashplayer)
- QuickTime (free download at www.apple.com/quicktime/download/)
- RealPlayer (free download at www.real.com/download/)
- Microsoft Office (available for purchase at http://office.microsoft.com/)
- Corel WordPerfect Office (available for purchase at www.wordperfect.com/)
- Oracle OpenOffice (free download at www.openoffice.org/; this software reads, writes, and converts Microsoft Office documents)

COMMON PLATFORMS FOR ONLINE CLASSES

Next we describe the most common LMSs, along with their features and some screenshots. Take this opportunity to familiarize yourself ahead of time with the LMS you will be using. Doing so will make your orientation with the class and its landscape that much easier. The information here is only preliminary, so visit the website for your LMS and read more, or complete a tutorial for the program.

Moodle

The Moodle LMS supports the following features (for more detailed information, you may want to visit www.moodle.org):

- Announcements
- Assignments
- Blogs (unedited news or comments)
- Calendar
- Chat (supports images)
- Course evaluations
- Discussion forum
- Gradebook
- Glossary
- Journal
- LMS Support (Moodle Help Desk)
- News
- Quiz
- Resources (external links, etc.)
- RSS feeds (frequently updated digital content)
- Survey
- Syllabus
- Wiki (shared, modifiable content page)
- Workshops (peer review and assessment)

Moodle can be customized, so before you start a course, always check to see what features are available in *your* Moodle LMS.

Figure 6.1 (see next page) represents a sample course home page in Moodle. The course you take may look a little different. This course home page includes a course menu, topic outline, activities, instructor notes, course announcements, news, upcoming events, and a course calendar.

Moodle is distributed to schools as "open source" software, which means there is no standard student interface. It is completely customizable for a school and its faculty members, so this snapshot of Moodle serves as a model of what a course *can* look like, but the course you take might vary. Because Moodle is customizable, all the features available are not necessarily used for every class, so be aware of the possible features available.

Moodle provides three standard options for the setup of the course: activities arranged by week, activities arranged by topic, or a discussion-focused social format. Your course will probably be organized in one of these three ways.

You can view discussions by date, by thread, or by author. Your posts in the classroom can include attachments, an image, or a URL. The discussion tool includes a formatting text editor. Posts may be peer-reviewed by your fellow students. A student may receive

Figure 6.1 Sample Course Home Page in Moodle. *Used with permission from Pearson Learning Solutions.*

posts to the discussion forums as daily digests of subject lines or whole posts as e-mail. You can subscribe to forum RSS (Really Simple Syndication) feeds, chunks of information based on preferences you submit.

The hardware requirements for Moodle include a basic personal computer running a standard operating system and a stable Internet connection. Moodle requires a browser supporting HTML 3.0 or higher (Microsoft Internet Explorer, Mozilla Firefox 3.0 or higher, Safari 5.0 or higher).

Figure 6.2 illustrates a sample Moodle lesson page. A lesson is called a *topic* or *weekly* in Moodle. Because Moodle is open source, the format of the lesson pages varies widely

Figure 6.2 Sample Moodle 2.0 Image from Moodle.org. *(Courtesy of Helen Foster, Moodle Community Manager—Revised by IAEGS). Used with permission from Pearson Learning Solutions.*

within a lesson. You can expect to find an overview, lesson objectives, reading assignments, lecture notes, and review exercises. Assignments and tests are handled separately. As with any course, regardless of LMS, whether or not a final proctored exam is required depends on the school offering the course. Always check before you start a course to see if a proctored exam is required and, if so, where it will be administered.

Take a few hours to explore all the parts of the course, including lessons, assignments, and lectures. Spending the time up front to figure out what is in the course and where it is located will pay off later on.

LearningStudio^{SM}

Figure 6.3 represents a sample course home page in LearningStudio^{SM} (formerly known as eCollege®). The type of content in each course is proprietary LMS content delivered primarily through pearsonlearningstudio.com or eCollege.com. Like other proprietary LMS packages, the user interface is standardized across installations. The course you take may have different graphic elements with various selectable color schemes, but navigation through the course is standard.

Figure 6.3 Sample Course Home Page in Learning Studio^{SM}. *Used with permission from David Ferguson and Learning Studio.*

The LearningStudio^{SM} LMS supports the following features (for more detailed information, you may want to visit www.pearsonlearningstudio.com):

- Announcements
- Assignments
- Calendar
- Chat
- Document sharing (with virus detection technology)
- Drop box (for assignment delivery and grading)
- E-mail/instant messaging
- Glossary

- Gradebook
- Group work
- Internal e-mail
- Journal
- Lecture (course content)
- Liveroom (synchronous communication interaction with whiteboard/chat/audio)
- Meeting (realtime meeting featuring video, app sharing, whiteboard)
- My Portfolio (personal portfolio and display folder)
- Quizzes
- Review
- RSS feeds
- Student home pages
- Syllabus
- Tasks
- Threaded discussion
- Voting (polling, surveys)
- Webliography (possible external links)
- Whiteboard

Students can download discussion group content into a format that can be printed or stored locally, as well as synchronize their address book and calendar events with a smartphone or PDA (personal digital assistant). Instructors can publish course content on a CD-ROM that can be linked dynamically from within the online course. Instructors can also record synchronous sessions so students can review them asynchronously at a later time, or publish course content on a CD-ROM for students who do not have Internet access.

LearningStudio^{SM} has an internal e-mail option. Students can use the e-mail feature to contact individuals and groups. Students can attach files and spell-check outgoing messages. They can also use a searchable address book to e-mail individuals and groups.

The chat tool within LearningStudio^{SM} supports private rooms and private messages. The system creates archive logs for all chat rooms. Instructors can schedule chats using the course calendar. The chat tool supports unlimited simultaneous group discussions.

In a LearningStudio^{SM} course, students have access to personal online calendars where they can track all their assignments, deadlines, and due dates. Students can view their grades on completed assignments and any instructor feedback, including total points earned, total points possible and percentages per unit, and overall course grade.

The software includes support for discussion forums. Discussions can be viewed by date, by thread, by author, by group, and by topics defined by the instructor. Instructors can associate a discussion with any course content. Instructors may create separate discussion environments for small groups and/or limit discussions to specific time periods. Only the instructor may delete posts, which can include attachments, images, or URLs. The entire discussion can be saved or printed for offline reading. Discussion threads are expandable and collapsible to view an entire conversation on one screen.

Students can submit assignments using drop boxes and can upload files to a shared course or group folder. Students can share the contents of their personal folders with their instructors. Instructors can upload files to the personal folder of a student. Virus detection technology is used throughout the file upload/download process.

The hardware requirements to run LearningStudio^SM include a basic personal computer running a standard Windows or Macintosh operating system and a stable Internet connection. LearningStudio^SM requires Microsoft Internet Explorer 7.0 or higher or Mozilla FireFox 3.0 or higher for Microsoft Windows. For Macintosh running OS X, Safari 3.0 or higher is required.

In the process of taking a course in LearningStudio^SM, you might be asked to view material written in a word processor format (MS Word, WordPerfect, OpenOffice, etc.). You also might be asked to submit materials in this format. So, before you start, make sure you have this type of software installed on your computer.

Figure 6.4 illustrates a sample LearningStudio^SM lesson page. Course lessons are called units in LearningStudio^SM. You can expect to find within a unit of a course a checklist, lesson objectives, reading assignments, lecture notes, activities, and review exercises. However, the content/layout of a unit can vary based on the requirements of the instructor.

Figure 6.4 Sample LearningStudio^SM Lesson Page. *Used with permission from David Ferguson and Learning Studio.*

Whether or not a proctored exam is required depends on the school offering the course. Always check before you start a course to see if a proctored exam is required and where it will be administered.

Blackboard

Before you delve into the details of Blackboard, it is interesting to note how this particular system evolved. Blackboard was initially designed to manage courses in a traditional/on-ground college environment. Rather than serving as a wholly online course method like most LMSs, it was intended as a tool to replace the massive amount of paper used to teach a face-to-face class and to provide students with constant feedback regarding their progress in the class.

Figure 6.5 represents a sample course home page in Blackboard. The type of content in each course differs, but the basic layout of the Blackboard interface is relatively standard across implementations. The screenshot here is a sample of what you see after you log on. Students can control which modules are visible (such as their report card, course catalog, alerts, etc.).

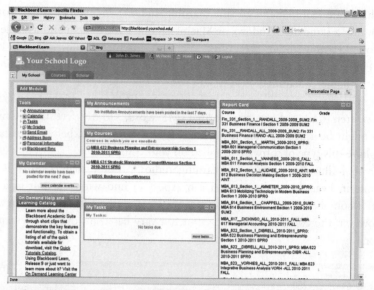

Figure 6.5 Sample Course Home Page in Blackboard. *Used with permission from David Ferguson and Blackboard.*

The Blackboard LMS supports the following (for more detailed information, you may want to visit www.blackboard.com):

- Address book
- Announcements
- Assignments
- Blogs
- Calendar
- Collaboration
- Digital drop box (student upload)
- Discussion board
- Echo360 (access to online video lectures)
- Virtual blackboard
- Glossary
- Gradebook
- Groups
- Journals (students' course and learning experiences)
- Messages (internal e-mail and instant messaging using Wimba)
- NBC Learn (access to NBC News archives)
- Quizzes
- Resources (external links, etc.)
- Roster
- RSS feeds
- Student home page
- Surveys
- Syllabus
- Tasks
- Wikis

The chat tool supports unlimited simultaneous group discussions and private messages. Instructors may moderate chats and suspend students from the chat rooms. The system creates archive logs for all chat rooms. Instructors can view chat logs and share these with students.

Discussions can be viewed by date and by thread. Instructors can associate a discussion with any course content. They can enable or disable anonymous postings and determine whether student posts are re-editable after they are first posted. Posts can contain URLs and file attachments, and they may contain HTML. The threaded discussion software includes a formatting text editor that can create mathematic equations. Instructors may create separate discussion environments for small groups of students and teaching assistants.

Students have a private folder where they can upload and download files, and instructors can upload files to the personal folder of a student. Students can upload files to a shared group folder, as well as submit assignments using drop boxes.

The hardware requirements to run Blackboard include a basic personal computer running a standard Windows or Macintosh operating system and a stable Internet connection. Blackboard requires a standard browser: Microsoft Windows XP (SP2 or higher), Vista, or 7 with Internet Explorer 7 or higher, Firefox 3.5 or higher; Mac OS X (10.2 or higher) with Safari 5.0 or higher, or Firefox 3.5 or higher.

Figure 6.6, illustrates a sample Blackboard assignment page. Within a lesson, you can expect to find the assignments, assignment materials, digital drop boxes, and so forth. The content/layout of a lesson can include any activity that is web viewable. Hence lesson presentation in Blackboard is nonstandard. Access to the content, however, is standard and available only through the "Course Content" link.

The Blackboard layout is uniform across courses and educational institutions, as are most commercial LMSs. Whether or not a final proctored exam is required depends on the school offering the course. Always check before you start a course to see if a proctored exam is required and where it will be administered.

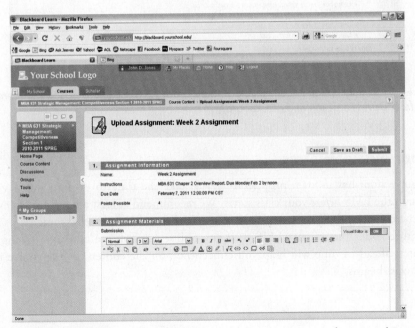

Figure 6.6 Sample Blackboard Assignment Page. *Used with permission from David Ferguson and Blackboard.*

Blackboard Learn ANGEL Edition®

To show you just how dynamic the online learning world is, since the first edition of this book, Blackboard Inc. acquired and merged with ANGEL Learning. Now, the features of Blackboard Inc. and ANGEL are together in one platform. Figure 6.7 shows a sample lesson page from the Blackboard Learn ANGEL Edition®.

The ANGEL Learning Management Suite (LMS) 7.4 supports the following additions to Blackboard's functionality (for more detailed information, you may want to visit www.blackboard.com/Platforms/Learn/Products/ANGEL-Edition.aspx):

- Mashups that make it easy to incorporate rich media content into courses from sources such as the YouTube™ website and Picasa™ software.

- Grading rubrics that ensure all manually graded submissions are evaluated against the same criteria.

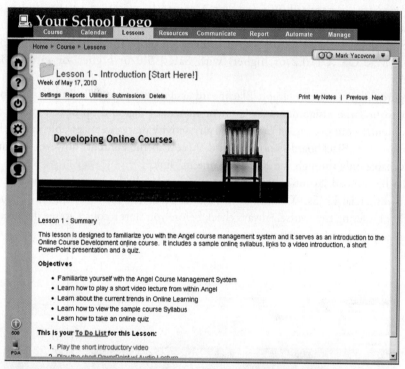

Figure 6.7 Sample Lesson Page from Blackboard Learn ANGEL Edition®. *Used with permission from David Ferguson and Blackboard.*

Proprietary Systems

If your school has its own proprietary LMS, take the time to explore and navigate through the LMS *before* your class starts. We recommend at least a few hours to examine the course and all its associated pieces. Find out if there is electronic or printed literature about the school's LMS or if any online tutorials are available. Doing this research ahead of time will help you concentrate on the content of the course itself once class begins.

MORE POWER
TO YOU

Now is your chance to explore this chapter's topics further. Check out the sites listed here. Enjoy expanding your knowledge and *more power to you*!

Moodle
www.moodle.org

LearningStudio^{SM}
www.pearsonlearningstudio.com

Blackboard
www.blackboard.com

Blackboard Learn ANGEL Edition®
www.blackboard.com/Platforms/Learn/Products/ANGEL-Edition.aspx

If any of these websites are not available or you wish to seek out additional information, we encourage you to do your own online search. Consider the concepts covered in the chapter that are most important to you, and think of various terms that could be used to describe them. For this chapter, some potential keywords to search include:

learning management systems

online learning platforms

When searching online, consider different ways to express ideas. Remember to use synonyms and related words. Try phrasing things in different ways. And always review more than the first few pages of search results.

For more specific information on searching online, refer to Chapter 10.

The Hybrid Balance

7

Understand that the terms *hybrid* or *blended* can mean various things in terms of how online and face-to-face classes are integrated.

Make sure you ask the right questions to determine exactly what kind of hybrid course your class is.

Determine how to best use your time for both the online and face-to-face portions of your hybrid course.

Recognize that hybrid courses ideally offer the best of both worlds—the benefits of online presentation technology and the personal interaction of the classroom.

Power UP

What is a hybrid course? Well, a good analogy (though perhaps not the most flattering one!) might explain it in terms of dogs.

WHAT KIND OF DOG IS THAT?

A dog that is a combination of breeds might be called a mutt, or a mixed-breed. In the same way, a course that combines online learning with some other way of presenting the material might be called blended, or hybrid, or mixed. Just as referring to a dog as a mutt doesn't tell you exactly what is in the mix—it could be a labradoodle, or it could be a husky/heeler/lab/schnauzer—calling a course hybrid doesn't tell you exactly what types of media, or how many, are combined. As mentioned in Chapter 1, a blended course generally has some online components and some on-ground components, but the exact mix can vary. Note: throughout this chapter, we will use the terms *hybrid* and *blended* interchangeably, just to reinforce the fact that there is no one name for this type of course. A hybrid course could be any of the following, and more:

- A 16-week course in which the majority of content and instruction is offered online, but there are two face-to-face workshops scheduled over specific weekends at the beginning—for orientation—and end—for conclusion—of the course.

- A course that alternates weekly between traditional classroom meetings and online meetings throughout the session.

- A course where content such as lectures and media like animations, movies, or simulations are offered online, and students attend class weekly to work in a learning lab where they practice, get help with problem areas, and take tests.

- A course that provides all basic instruction online, but offers an in-person meeting for students every 2 weeks, for questions, student presentations, and in-depth discussion.

If you do a search online for *blended learning*, you will find there are a multitude of definitions. For our purposes, as long as the course combines online learning with in-person classroom time in some way, it is considered blended. Whether a course is hybrid or not has no impact on how long it is, the level (100, 200, 300, etc.), whether it is synchronous or asynchronous, how many students might be in the class, what LMS is used, or whether it uses e-books or not. Hybrid is purely a matter of how the course is staged. Taking a hybrid course will require the same computer resources as taking an all-online course.

As illustrated in the examples listed, the occurrence of face-to-face class time can happen in many ways. Sometimes the on-ground class meetings occur only at the beginning and the end of the course. Sometimes they are placed at particular points so that coverage of specific course content has the benefit of face-to-face discussion. And other times, the in-person class meetings simply alternate with the online meetings.

Figure 7.1 helps illustrate the variety of factors that can work together in varying degrees to create a blended course.

There is also a lesser-known, specialized version of blended learning known as *hyflex*. The word combines the terms *hybrid* and *flexible*. Courses of this type are set up so that the online course and the traditional classroom course are offered in unison, and students can choose which content they attend class for and which they pursue online at their own discretion. In a hyflex course, students might attend class online—unless they conveniently happen to be in the area of the campus at the time of class. Or they might attend almost wholly on campus—except when business travel requirements mean that online attendance is the only way to keep up. As you can imagine, a course of this type must be completely aligned, since it is in essence two sessions of the exact same course offered at the exact same time, just in different modalities.

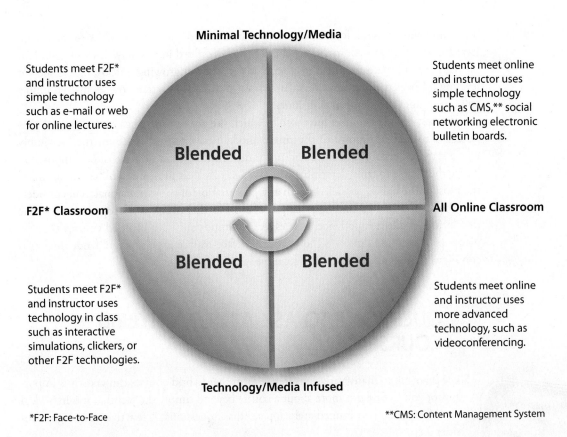

Minimal Technology/Media

Students meet F2F* and instructor uses simple technology such as e-mail or web for online lectures.

Students meet online and instructor uses simple technology such as CMS,** social networking electronic bulletin boards.

Blended   Blended

F2F* Classroom   All Online Classroom

Blended   Blended

Students meet F2F* and instructor uses technology in class such as interactive simulations, clickers, or other F2F technologies.

Students meet online and instructor uses more advanced technology, such as videoconferencing.

Technology/Media Infused

*F2F: Face-to-Face

**CMS: Content Management System

Figure 7.1 Variations of Blended Learning Programs

Source: Blended Learning: A Report on the ELI Focus Session. Veronica Diaz, Associate Director, EDUCAUSE Learning Initiative, Malcolm Brown, Director, EDUCAUSE Learning Initiative. ELI Paper 2: 2010, November 2010. Used under the conditions of EDUCAUSE Creative Commons License, which applies only to this screenshot.

WHY HYBRID?

The reasons schools offer hybrid courses are many. In some cases, they do it to address space issues—offering blended courses means school administration can optimize limited classroom space. Offering a hybrid course can also open it up to a wider audience. And in other cases, a course may be put in hybrid form because it has been determined that the content can best be covered through leveraging different modalities.

As you might imagine, students attend hybrid courses for many reasons as well. Sometimes a particular course is not offered any other way. Sometimes students just want to stick closer to "the norm" of classroom learning while dipping a toe into the new world of online learning. Sometimes students—and instructors—see the value of online learning but want the social interaction that traditional classroom teaching provides. You can probably think of some subjects (math is a common one) where firsthand interaction with an expert makes a big difference. Sometimes there are nuances to a topic that only in-person communication can get across. Some schools single out particular courses to be designed specifically in hybrid form because the combination of online and on-ground classwork has shown to be an optimal way to teach the content.

According to the U.S. Department of Education, there were approximately 1 million enrollments in blended courses during the 2006–2007 school year. Much research supports the fact that students often have higher achievement and higher satisfaction in blended-learning courses. However, this is not something that can be taken for granted because, as discussed previously, blended learning does not have one set meaning. In general though, it is safe to say that the results of blended-learning studies have been positive.

The compelling reasons for schools to offer blended courses and students to take them have led to steady growth in the number of courses offered in this way. The exact amount of that growth is hard to quantify—some surveys show it growing quickly, others show it leveling off over the past few years. And most research shows that courses offered online still outnumber blended-learning courses.

The best blended courses are those in which the entire course has been designed purposefully to take advantage of the mixed modalities. Courses where instructors simply take a standard classroom course and put some of the content on a website, without analyzing the course to truly determine which aspects are best presented online, do not make the most of the hybrid model. As with any presentation of educational material, considerable thought should go into how the pieces of a blended course work together to provide the optimal student experience. It is especially important with blended courses that the pieces of the course "mesh." The online and face-to-face aspects should not offer two completely different courses, but a cohesive whole.

QUESTIONS TO ASK ABOUT A HYBRID COURSE

Since there are so many variations in the form that hybrid courses can take, it is important for you to find out more about a course beyond simply the fact that it *is* hybrid. If the information isn't immediately apparent, ask questions. A few that you might consider are:

- How is the hybrid course split between online and classroom presentation of content?
- How is attendance measured?
- Where are class meetings located?
- What parts of the course are online, and what does the instructor focus on in the on-ground classroom?

As with mixed-breed dogs, some hybrid courses mix the types of instruction more successfully than others. We will say again what we said in Chapter 1: For any course, multiple factors make the difference in whether it is "good," including the quality of the instruction, the teacher, and the organization of the class. You will have to decide what makes a class "better" for you based on your own goals and priorities. But ideally, blended courses offer the best of both worlds—they provide rich, diverse instruction and they allow the students to access basic content on their own time and to practice 21st-century skills, while still providing expert in-person facilitation. They allow instructors to spend valuable class time being responsive to student questions and problems rather than reciting rote lectures.

FINDING YOUR OWN HYBRID BALANCE

In the same way that you need to put thought into how you will approach a 100% online course in terms of timing, you need to be thoughtful about how you approach a blended course. With a blended course, a few more factors are thrown into the mix that you will need to plan around. If planning for an online course means considering when you will log in to class and how you will schedule your work online and off, then taking a hybrid course means you need to consider what aspects of the course are offered when and how you will adjust your own work to the best advantage. In one scenario:

- your best use of time online may be to review material and participate in discussion,

- your best use of time in the classroom may be to ask questions of the instructor and other students and obtain feedback,

- and your best use of time offline and out of class may be to read and study the material.

But since every hybrid course is different, you will need to analyze each situation and determine how you can use the flexibility of blended learning to make sure you get the most out of the course.

Though well-designed blended courses can be an ideal way to learn, you have to keep in mind the same factors as with any instruction: If the content, activities, assessments, and instruction are all well designed, you are likely to learn a lot and have a good experience. But if any one of those factors falls short, it can be a serious issue. Recognize that if a single blended course didn't turn out well—on account of a weak instructor, or poorly designed assessments, or any other reason—it doesn't mean you should consign all courses of that type to the rubbish heap. Every class is different, and you have to give blended learning more than a single chance to figure out whether it works for you. Especially for students who have been dissatisfied with 100% online courses and desire more personal interaction, blended courses can be the right choice. It is worth it to experiment by taking a blended course to determine whether this style of instruction is your new favorite way to learn.

MORE POWER TO YOU

Now is your chance to further explore the topics of Chapter 7. Check out the sites listed here. Enjoy expanding your knowledge, and *more power to you!*

Are Hybrid Courses for Me?
www4.uwm.edu/ltc/hybrid/student_resources/for_me.cfm

Hybrid Courses: Obstacles and Solutions for Faculty and Students
www.uwex.edu/disted/conference/Resource_library/proceedings/03_72.pdf

Hybrid Course Gallery
www.mcli.dist.maricopa.edu/ocotillo/hybrids/gallery.php

Comments from Online/Hybrid Students
www.drexel.edu/engphil/online8.asp

If any of these websites are not available or you wish to seek out additional information, we encourage you to do your own online search. Consider the concepts covered in the chapter that are most important to you, and think of various terms that could be used to describe them. For this chapter, some potential keywords to search include:

hybrid courses

blended learning

hyflex

When searching online, consider different ways to express ideas. Remember to use synonyms and related words. Try phrasing things in different ways. And always review more than the first few pages of search results.

For more specific information on searching online, refer to Chapter 10.

Communicating Online: Who, What, When, How, and Why

Power UP

⏻ Understand that synchronized communication occurs when we all talk and listen to each other at the same time.

⏻ Understand that asynchronized communication occurs when participation in a conversation is spaced out over time.

⏻ Know and follow basic e-mail communication guidelines.

⏻ Address various online communication concerns such as language, listening, and appropriateness.

⏻ Follow appropriate guidelines for responding to messages in the online classroom.

⏻ Differentiate the various forms of online communication, including forums, newsgroups, chat rooms, wikis, and blogs.

Because it is easy for everyone to get involved, the online learning environment offers a rich and diverse experience. Unlike on-ground classrooms, one or two people cannot easily dominate an online class. Everyone is expected to respond to every question, and thus participation is much more equitable.

In an online course, you have the opportunity to make connections with other students in various states and time zones, maybe even different countries. Communication in the online environment puts few limits on time and place. The classroom environment is also considered far less intimidating than a face-to-face classroom because almost all communication takes place from your own computer in your own comfortable space.

You can communicate online by using a variety of tools and avenues. Following are the more common ones you will probably be exposed to as you begin and continue your online adventure:

- E-mail
- Forums/newsgroups
- Chat rooms
- Wikis and blogs

E-MAIL

Almost everyone uses electronic mail these days. Proper computer etiquette is essential to communicate well online. Use these strategies when you are communicating in your virtual classroom.

E-mail Communication Guidelines

Even if you do not consider yourself a writer, as an online student, you will be. And there are certain conventions and considerations to keep in mind to make your writing clear, readable, and inoffensive.

Wallpaper

Avoid background wallpaper or setting your messages up to look like electronic stationery for online messages and e-mails. Although it may look fancy, it can make messages hard to read and actually slows things down between systems because wallpaper takes up more space in the computer's memory.

Fonts

Although you have many options, there are certainly some fonts that are more acceptable than others when sending messages. Avoid using an offbeat or unusual font, even if you think it is expressive of your personality. It may be difficult for others to read. If all reading is done on-screen, stick with sans serif fonts (like this). Serif fonts (like this) are easier to read on a hard-copy page.

Make sure your font size is in the middle and readable range, generally 12 point. Large or small fonts may make reading more difficult for others, depending on their screen size and the keenness of their eyesight.

Color

Although it can be fun and interesting to use different font and background colors, resist the temptation. Some color combinations work better than others: a dark font on a light background is always easier to read and more professional.

Avoid high-contrast colors. For instance, stay away from blue text on an orange background. Colors should have medium tone or brightness so they show up but are not overwhelming on the screen.

As people age, the color red becomes harder to distinguish, so avoid using red for large sections of text.

All Caps

Do not use all caps. In an online environment, using capital letters conveys YELLING LOUDLY. In addition, depending on the length of your message, writing in all caps makes your message difficult to read on-screen.

Emoticons

Emoticons are simple graphics used to enhance your message by indicating emotion. They are best used to be sure you clearly convey your intentions whenever you use humor, anger, or a subtle emotion in a message or posting.

Some people use the winking emoticon to denote humor: ;)

Another popular emoticon is the unhappy face to denote something sad in a message:

Do not overuse emoticons because they can make your messages seem silly or shallow. However, when used sparingly, they can put your point across and express the appropriate tone.

Note: For any of the word-processing functions just discussed, if you do not know how to manipulate fonts, colors, and the rest, ask a classmate or friend, use the tutorials included in the program, or do a search online for information on formatting documents specific to your word-processing program.

Spelling and Punctuation

Spelling and punctuation are just as crucial in an online environment as in a hard-copy business letter. You want to come across as an educated person. Although you may not be graded on your grammar and spelling in online discussion, it will certainly affect people's perceptions of you. Poor spelling and grammar skills lead others to lower expectations regarding your intelligence and professionalism. Further, your intended message may be misconstrued, at the very least. Just as you are probably careful when communicating verbally to use the appropriate words, think the same way online! And use the tools available in your software and in your LMS, such as the spell-checker.

Abbreviations

Any of you who send text messages know there are many common abbreviations (ttfn = ta-ta for now; ttyl = talk to you later, etc.). But for classroom communication, you need to be more formal and avoid slang abbreviations.

Also, clarity is important, and not everyone is familiar with these abbreviations. It is best to write out terms in the more conventional way. In the end, though, your instructor will set the tone for the class, so pay attention and follow his or her lead about the level of formality of language. When using more traditional abbreviations or acronyms, present the full word or phrase at least once before using the abbreviation or acronym.

In your online communication, be courteous, concise, and positive, but try to express your personality in your writing. You do not want to sound dry or like a robot. It may take you a while to find your voice online, but try to reach a level where your online communication is similar in tone to your voice communication in an on-ground classroom.

Other Online Communication Concerns

Reading Between the Lines

Communication is complex, whether written or spoken. When you do not have visual and auditory cues, you can easily misconstrue people's comments. You do not have the same nonverbal cues to reference in an online environment as you do face to face, but you can still gain insight into people's communication.

Different people have different styles. Pay attention to how people express themselves, and you will begin to have a sense of their thoughts beyond just their words as you get to know them. But be cautious in your interpretations. Your own moods and preconceived notions can influence the way you interpret other people's communication. Usually, we can assume all messages are intended in a friendly, professional way, unless strong indicators within the message itself point in another direction.

Learning to Listen Online

In a classroom setting, you wouldn't have the TV on or children running around. If you are working in the online classroom, though, there may be numerous distractions in the environment. Try to limit the background noise in the area where you are working and really focus so you can read online content accurately.

For some people, listening to music is not a distraction; for others, any noise disrupts their attention. Do what you need to make your environment work for you so you can focus and process the online content. Consider this: If all you have to add to a discussion is "I agree," maybe you didn't listen or process well enough.

Quality of Responses

Keep in mind that the online communications in your class may be archived for a long time. Any time you misspell a word or say something foolish, your words may live on to haunt you. Take the opportunity to think before you post a message to the class. One good approach is to create all your responses in a separate document and take the time to reread and fine-tune them before you upload them for all the world to see.

However, we do encourage you not to avoid responding because you are intimidated. Too much thought might mean you decide not to post a piece that would lead to a great discussion. Again, there is a fine line. Here is an example:

Let's say a fellow student made a comment about his boss that made you think the student was the problem, not the boss. You would want to respond. So do not talk yourself out of it, but think how you can get your point across without contributing to the problem or hurting feelings. You might say something like, "the boss you are describing in this situation does sound like someone with whom I may not wish to work, but I also think a lot about things from the other perspective. What would the boss say? Maybe he is very stressed and unhappy, and you just pushed his buttons."

E-mail Addresses: Keep It Professional

During your program, you will need an e-mail account. Most of the time, your e-mail account is school sponsored. Be careful about the names you use because others will see them. Do you really want your e-mail to be sexymama@schoolname.edu? Choose your e-mail address name wisely and make it simple and tasteful. We recommend "your first name your last name@schoolname.edu." It is easy to remember and, most importantly, clear and professional.

Knowing What Not to Share: Personal Information

Surprisingly, in an online environment, people tend to share more, rather than less, information. Sometimes people share too much, disclosing inappropriate details regarding intimate personal subjects in the guise of responding to course questions or assignments. Perhaps this problem relates to the anonymity factor, or perhaps people just get carried away. So keep in mind: Monitor your own communication and try to keep your communication appropriate. Steer away from private disclosure unless personal revelations are the specific focus of an assignment. Your instructor and classmates are wonderful resources, but they are not personal counselors.

Be aware that although you may want to talk about your employer and your job experiences, you should be careful about the information you divulge. Many companies have policies regarding disclosing proprietary information. Lastly, consider what contact information is appropriate. Some students create a signature line and include their phone number. Do you really want your phone number available on every single message you send? Your communication in the online classroom should be professional and courteous rather than soul-baring.

Review of Synchronized and Asynchronized Communication

Synchronized communication occurs when we are all talking and listening to each other at the same time, whether in a classroom, or over the phone, or through a virtual meeting. Everyone is engaged and participating in the communication at the same time.

Asynchronized communication occurs when we are not all engaged in the conversation at the same time, even though we are all participating. For instance,

- The old-fashioned exchange of letters among pen pals
- E-mail
- Exchanging voice mails
- Participating in an online discussion in which one person responds at 8 A.M. and is offline by 9 P.M., and someone else doesn't respond until he comes online from 11 P.M. until 2 A.M.

Whether your course interactions are synchronized or asynchronized depends on the institution and the instructor. Be aware of the nature of any specific communication situation. If it is asynchronized, you probably have more time to review your responses. Consider giving others a chance to respond to your initial postings before you come back for more. The point of online discussions is to hear more than one voice, and the input of others may give you more food for thought.

Threading Responses in the Classroom

You must deal with a large number of messages every day in the online classroom. You can help others manage the sometimes overwhelming number of messages by creating messages considerately. These are simple actions that will set a good example for everyone in your online classroom. Here are some examples.

1. *Use an appropriate subject line.* During the course of a conversation, the topic often changes. Therefore, if the subject line reads "Week Two-DQ1" and the conversation has evolved to a discussion on time management, change the subject line. You should be able to maintain the thread with a new subject line without a problem.

2. *Place your message first when replying to someone's message.* The newest addition to the conversation needs to be the first thing read. Then be sure to include the relevant sections of the previous message, or even the entire previous message,

so people can follow the conversation. Readers can then elect to read further if they need a reminder about what has gone on before. If the older messages are placed first and the newest at the bottom, readers are forced not only to scroll down to read the latest comment but also they must skim the notes previously read.

3. ***Be attentive to the appearance of your notes.***   As mentioned earlier, avoid fonts that are difficult to read because of style, color, or size. The format should not be more important than the content. Keep in mind when reading on the computer screen that long paragraphs are difficult to follow. As a general rule, limit each paragraph in an e-mail message to five to seven lines if possible.

4. ***Reduce confusion by considering a variety of methods of replying.***   Although most often a straightforward reply is appropriate, sometimes you can intersperse comments on each point in the original message, increasing the readability of your response.

5. ***Exercise good editing techniques.***   In threaded discussions, editing of notes refers to removing those portions of the message to which you are replying that are unnecessary to understand your comments. Although it is important to include enough of the previous message(s) to place the note in context, you will seldom need to include the entire message. It is frustrating to download lengthy messages that include dozens of messages already read, and it is equally annoying to download a message that mentions research but contains no references whatsoever.

FORUMS/NEWSGROUPS

Forums and newsgroups are essentially worldwide bulletin systems, made up of individuals chatting virtually about a particular topic in synchronous time. Forums and newsgroups can be about any topic.

For instance, if you are having a particularly hard time with a final paper, you can create a forum. Perhaps call it "final paper discussion." This will be a place where students are able to talk about their challenges regarding the final paper and strategies to make the paper easier to write, as well as inviting general comments on the final paper. The positive brainstorming and synergy that can come out of forums and newsgroups is substantial and a great resource for online students.

CHAT ROOMS

Chat rooms are virtual rooms where casual conversations with your peers can take place. They are for two or more people to have a text-based dialogue. Most major course management systems, such as the ones outlined in Chapter 6, have chat room capabilities. Chat rooms are not only used educationally, but they are also available on many popular Internet portal sites.

For instructional purposes, chat rooms can be used for the following: small group meetings, brainstorming with your classmates, virtual office hours with your professor, and study review sessions.

Pros for Chat Rooms

• Chats can be recorded, archived, and posted for future viewing.

• Chats can allow real-time communication, which can be faster than e-mail or posted discussion in the classroom.

- Chat rooms are an excellent way to connect with your classmates outside of the classroom.

Cons for Chat Rooms

- The fast environment can make some people feel uncomfortable and overwhelmed.
- Individuals with limited English proficiency or below-average typing skills may not adjust well to the fast-paced environment.
- Chat room conversation can be hard to follow when everyone is chatting at once. Just like any conversation in person, if you are being interrupted it may be difficult to finish your thought.

 # WIKIS AND BLOGS

The term *wiki* is derived from a Hawaiian term for "fast." A wiki is a collaborative online database in the form of a website that allows visitors to join in the adding, removing, and editing of content.

Wikis are an extremely democratic way of presenting information because anyone can participate. However, this same open access means that wikis are not always reliable sources. The people who post information may be experts in the field or they may not. They may have the best intentions of presenting the truth on a topic or they may not. Be wary of the content of wikis, and always look for corroboration on wiki content from more reputable sources.

Blog is short for "web log." A blog is a running chronological journal of personal thoughts posted online. A blog may include proprietary multimedia content such as pictures, video, or audio, as well as links to information and other sites available on the Internet. Blogs exist on any and every topic, and they are generally updated regularly. Some people use blogs in the same way as diaries or personal journals; others use them more as editorials or forums to express their opinions on specific topics such as politics or music. Blogs may have restricted or limited access to outsiders, or they may be public sites. Some public blogs even provide a source of income for their authors, through posted advertisements.

The rapid evolution of technology is constantly impacting the way we communicate with one another. The specific technologies utilized in your class will depend on your school and your instructor.

MORE POWER ———— TO YOU

Now is your chance to explore this chapter's topics further. Check out the sites listed here. Enjoy expanding your knowledge and *more power to you!*

Virtual Communication
http://hbswk.hbs.edu/archive/2122.html

Netiquette
www.studygs.net/netiquette.htm

Blog
www.marketingterms.com/dictionary/blog/

Got Something to Say?
www.livingdot.com/

Wikipedia
www.wikipedia.org/

If any of these websites are not available or you wish to seek out additional information, we encourage you to do your own online search. Consider the concepts covered in the chapter that are most important to you, and think of various terms that could be used to describe them. For this chapter, some potential terms to search by include:

netiquette

document formatting basics

e-mail guidelines

When searching online, consider different ways to express ideas. Remember to use synonyms and related words. Try phrasing things in different ways. And always review more than the first few pages of search results.

For more specific information on searching online, refer to Chapter 10.

Working in the
Online Classroom

Recognize that most people find it more difficult to read from a computer monitor than hard copy. Be careful and focused when you read text on-screen.

Understand that being a good reader doesn't mean you read fast. A good reader is one who understands and processes the information being presented.

Know that typing will be the medium for all your communication in an online environment. Evaluate your typing skills. If they are at all weak, seek to improve.

Identify the qualities of good writing. Improve your own writing through increasing your reading, obtaining feedback, and doing more writing.

Be aware that poor writing skills will impact your grade, regardless of the course subject. If your writing skills are weak, seek to improve.

Although the online learning environment shares many similarities with the traditional on-ground classroom environment, numerous factors set online learning apart from other instructional mediums. Some of the differences are not obvious; others are plain to see. In this chapter, we review the factors you need to consider when working in the online classroom.

READING IN AN ONLINE ENVIRONMENT

Although it may not be obvious, there is a difference between reading text on a computer screen and reading text on paper. Reading on-screen is generally harder on your eyes and can result in blurring, eyestrain, and visual fatigue (Rhodes, 1998).

Most people do not read as quickly or efficiently from a computer monitor as they do when reading hard copy. Evaluate your own skill level. If you are not a strong reader, you might print out any important text so you can read it on paper. Having the hard copy gives you the opportunity to make notes or highlight within the document, which can be very helpful to your learning and retention. Some software has this capability too and may be an option worth exploring.

Do not make the mistake of thinking that a good reader equates to being a fast reader. Reading effectively means you understand and process the information presented, however much time it takes.

Online reading requires scrolling down the page to follow the text, which can irritate your eyes as you track the moving text. In addition, it is quite easy to miss whole passages of text if you are not careful as you scroll down a web page.

Some schools take this into consideration and try to minimize the need for scrolling in their materials. But even if you are fortunate enough to be in a class where only short passages are placed on-screen, you are bound to run across overlong passages. There will probably always be the need for some scrolling.

Thus you must be careful and focused when you read text on-screen. Pay close attention to where you are on the page, as well as what the text is actually saying.

Printing out every bit of information can result in lots of paper waste. If this concerns you, or if printing everything out is not an option, consider reading pertinent passages on the computer more than one time to ensure you process the information. Good reading skills are one of the keys to your success as an online student, so do all you can to optimize and improve your skills.

TYPING SKILLS: A NECESSITY

Whether you are a good or a poor typist, you *will* be a typist if you are an online student. Typing skills are almost as important as reading skills for an online learner. In a traditional classroom, you might be able to get away with typing only when you have an assignment due. But in an online environment, you are typing all of the time. Typing will be the medium for *all* your communication, so you need to polish your skills if you are at all weak. Being a reasonably fast, accurate typist can make a real difference in the time it takes you to respond to questions and complete assignments, both on the initial writing and on the editing and correcting of errors.

Even today when typing on the computer keyboard is common, many people still type with the hunt-and-peck or two-finger method. What matters is not whether you have had formal training in typing, but whether you are efficient and effective. Some people who hunt and peck are faster than others who type in the traditional manner. Determine whether your typing skills could be improved, and consider the following options: online typing programs, software packages, library books, or typing courses at local schools and colleges. Good typing skills will contribute to making you a successful online student.

WRITING SKILLS: PRACTICE MAKES PERFECT

How well do you write? Undoubtedly, you will write a great deal during your academic career. You will have essays, papers, maybe even poems to create. If you are a strong writer, congratulations! If you are not, now is the time to improve your skills. You may have the most revolutionary new idea that ever occurred to anyone, but if you cannot express it competently and concisely in writing, it will not be recognized.

Poor writing skills will impact your grade, regardless of the course subject. There are as many ways to describe the qualities necessary for good writing as there are writers, but in general, good writing has the following qualities:

- *Correct spelling.* If you are a poor speller, you know it by now. Take advantage of the spell-checker. Ask someone who is a good speller to check your work if you can.

- *Proper grammar and punctuation.* Know and apply the rules for grammar and punctuation. If you need help, refer to the style guide for your school or invest in a grammar handbook.

- *Appropriate word choice.* If you have a good vocabulary, use it. If you do not, start developing it. Avoid slang. Strive for clarity and conciseness. Use language that is correct for the audience, the subject, and the circumstances.

- *Variable sentence structure.* Sentences should vary in length and structure between simple and complex. Use various techniques to help the text flow.

- *Logical organization.* Good writing sets up ideas in a logical, understandable order. The point of the writing is clear, and relevant details and examples obviously support the main idea. A particular format is followed as required. If you are in doubt, use an outline to structure your thoughts.

- *A unique style.* Good writers are professional while still letting their own distinct personality come through into their writing.

Always be sure to proofread your work so you can catch any errors in the areas just outlined. One simple, yet effective, proofreading technique is to read your work aloud slowly and listen carefully for awkward phrases or transitions. You may also want to have a family member or friend read your work or read your paper to them. You can also find numerous resources in the library, the bookstore, and online, with advice and practice exercises for polishing your writing skills. If you know your writing skills are weak, start to work on them now.

Improve Your Writing by Reading

The more you read, the better writer you will become. Try to read more and to read more diverse types of material. Challenge yourself in the areas of vocabulary and subject matter, and you will see your own thinking processes and vocabulary improve. If you do not read, it is likely you are not a great writer, and you will stay that way until you increase your reading. No matter what your interests, books and periodicals are available that address them.

Find motivation, and start reading more. It will expand your mind and improve your writing skills.

Improve Your Writing by Practicing

Of course, the more you write, the better writer you will become. Here are some ways to improve:

- Keep a journal. It is a great way to practice your writing skills and find your voice.

- Find someone who is a good writer to review your work and give you feedback.

- Keep in mind that good writers seldom finish anything in one draft. It takes multiple drafts to arrive at a well-written product. Expect to go through consecutive drafts of any writing assignment. Each draft will be an improvement over the last. And the more time you spend, the better your final product is likely to be.

Your instructors will probably vary in how much they emphasize writing skills. Keep in mind that, just like students, instructor skill levels vary. Those instructors who are not strong writers are unlikely to give you much constructive feedback. Those who have high-level writing skills will be the most critical when it comes to evaluating student writing. If you are fortunate enough to have an instructor who offers constructive criticism, take advantage of it. Learn as much as you can. You might even ask if he or she would be willing to review your papers for other classes. The instructor might not have the time, but it never hurts to ask.

Improving your reading, writing, and typing skills will serve you well for all your online courses. Plus, the added bonus is that polishing these skills will also benefit you in your career.

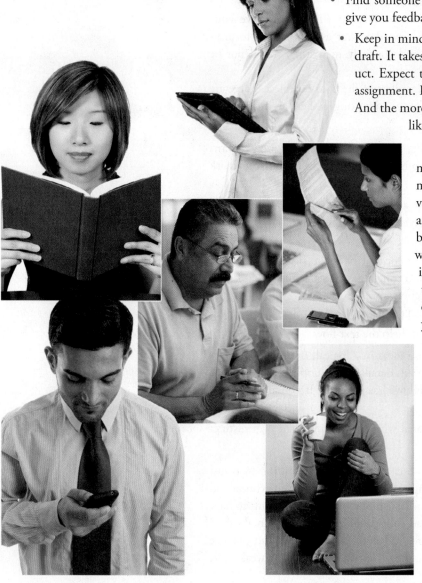

Reading more will help improve your writing skills.

MORE POWER
TO YOU

Now is your chance to explore this chapter's topics further. Check out the sites listed here. Enjoy expanding your knowledge and *more power to you*!

Reading Comprehension Lessons

www.readingcomprehensionconnection.com/

The Art of Close Reading: Parts 1–3

www.criticalthinking.org/articles/sts-ct-art-close-reading-p1.cfm
www.criticalthinking.org/articles/sts-ct-art-close-reading-p2.cfm
www.criticalthinking.org/articles/sts-ct-art-close-reading-p3.cfm

Typing Practice

www.learn2type.com

Only Typing Games

www.onlytypinggames.com/

If any of these websites are not available or you wish to seek out additional information, we encourage you to do your own online search. Consider the concepts covered in the chapter that are most important to you, and think of various terms that could be used to describe them. For this chapter, some potential keywords to search include:

online reading skills

typing tutorial

writing skills

When searching online, consider different ways to express ideas. Remember to use synonyms and related words. Try phrasing things in different ways. And always review more than the first few pages of search results.

For more specific information on searching online, refer to Chapter 10.

Thinking and Researching Online

10

Examine your thinking process. Pay attention. Try to think more deeply about the information presented in class by translating it into your own words, making connections, and asking questions.

Be aware that the basis of critical thinking is questioning. Ask thoughtful questions. Remember not to take information at face value. Consider other perspectives.

Understand what search engines are and how to use them.

Be a critical researcher. Don't assume everything you find on the web is accurate. Dig deeper.

Understand the serious offense of plagiarism. Avoid plagiarizing by always citing your sources correctly and completely.

Although you have undoubtedly had experiences in which you had to research and think things through, researching online requires particular strategies and methods. This chapter covers the most important techniques.

THINKING ABOUT COURSE CONTENT

Thinking is internally processing the information presented to you. Here are some ways to help you really think about the concepts presented in your class:

- Relate the new information to your own experiences or what you've already learned.

- Translate the concepts into your own words. What related ideas and information does the new content bring to mind? Be sure to take note of any questions that occur to you regarding the ideas presented in class.

- *Do not* parrot the text or the responses of your classmates. Use your own background knowledge and experiences to contribute to what you are reading and learning. How might the concepts being discussed in class apply to you? Keep an open mind.

- Try to have a holistic as well as a personal view. How do these ideas impact your life as well as the greater world?

- Pay attention to your thought process. Try to communicate in your writing *how* your ideas progress from one point to the other. Think of working out a math problem. It is helpful for you and others to be able to see the process. This approach not only shows your instructor how you are thinking through the concepts, but it can be helpful to your classmates as an example of a way to approach their learning.

- Ask questions. Seek clarity about the goals of individual assignments and activities, and try to ensure that what you take away from an assignment matches the learning objective.

- We all learn from one another. Pay attention to the comments and insights of your instructor, as well as your classmates. Use their diverse knowledge and perspectives to round out and contribute to your own. Don't forget to give credit to others for their ideas!

Critical Thinking

The basis of critical thinking is questioning, which can help you achieve clarity regarding what is being said, as well as why and how. Here are some questions to consider:

- Is this correct according to what I already know?
- Who is saying it and why?
- Who is the intended audience for this information?
- What perspective is being put forward?
- What other perspectives might be relevant?
- What sounds right about this to you and what sounds wrong, and why?
- Why would someone want you to believe this?
- What other questions does this information provoke?

    Try to remember not to just take information at face value.

Ask Questions

Don't be afraid to ask questions, even if you do not obtain sufficient answers. Just the asking can help you gain clarity about the important concepts. Questioning is also a valuable way to decipher your own views about the information presented in class. Even if you think you know the answer, you may want to ask the question just to check your thoughts or possibly learn a different take on the subject.

Remember, asking questions does not mean just interrogating your instructor and classmates. It also means being open to letting others question you. It even means questioning your own opinions and preconceived notions and trying to determine their origins truthfully. Responding thoughtfully to others' questions can also clarify your own reasoning.

INTERNET RESEARCH

Critical thinking is especially important with regard to Internet research. Thinking about an idea and approaching it from different angles will aid you in doing online searches. Also, being critical of the information presented will help you sift through the vast amount of data on the web and determine which online sources are relevant and reliable for your purposes.

Search Engines

Search engines are the tools you use on the web to lead you to information. You are probably already familiar with a few of them. If you have online access you may already use Google, bing, Alta Vista, Ask.com, or Yahoo!

A search engine typically features a page with a box where you type in words to describe the information you want. Type in the word(s), hit return, and the "engine" searches the Internet for mentions of those particular word(s). If you are unfamiliar with search engines, go to Google.com and experiment with searching. Use any tutorials or help information offered.

How and where a particular engine searches can vary. Some search engines look for specific forms of information, such as scholarly materials, while others are more general.

Technically, search engines can be categorized into two types: individual search engines and metasearch engines.

• Individual search engines are the most basic ones. They search the whole web.

• Metasearch engines are those that search, and usually organize, the results from other search engines.

Decide what type of search engine is right for your purposes before you begin your research.

Types of Online Searches

You can do a basic, uncomplicated web search using an engine such as Google just by directly typing in the relevant terms. There are two tricks to effective searching of this type: language options and persistence.

You need to think critically about your topic and come at it from various angles, using different words and giving yourself language options. Putting together a successful online search is a little like note taking. The best way to do it is not just to copy out exact words from the lecture or text but to grasp the main ideas and restate them in your own language. It is a game in word association, and it helps to have a wide vocabulary, a creative thought process, and a knowledge of synonyms. For instance, say you are searching for information regarding *online learning*. Of course, your obvious initial search terms are those words. But try varying the words. What other terms would express the same concept or something closely related? For "online" you might consider *computer*, or *distance*, or even *virtual*. For "learning" you might try *learner*, or *classroom*, or *student*. Mixing up and recombining all these different, but similar, terms will give you some more interesting and diverse search results than just the basic concept you started with. And if you can't think of various terms right away, do that initial search using *online learning*, and see what other related terms are included in the results list from that search to give you additional ideas.

The element of persistence comes into the equation in two ways. Try numerous different word combinations before being satisfied with your results. And do not limit yourself to finding information in the first few pages of results that come up. Skim through three to five pages of the results, especially if nothing really relevant seems to have come from the search. Sometimes the good stuff is buried further down the list.

Although you can always do a search as just described by typing any terms into the engine that are relevant to what you want to find, the Internet does offer more complex options. You might need to use a specific type of search method to find exactly what you are looking for. Two basic types of online searches that give you more finesse are Boolean and Wildcard.

Boolean Searches

A Boolean search uses the terms *and*, *or*, and/or *not* to set particular limits on the information being searched. Boolean is the type of logic used in these searches. It defines the relationship among the terms used in the search. Boolean logic takes its name from the British-born Irish mathematician and philosopher George Boole.

The easiest way to envision what you are doing when you use a Boolean search is to show it through Venn diagrams. Observe the following examples:

Using the term OR in a Boolean search

    Goal: I would like information about college.

    Query: college OR university

In this search, you will retrieve records in which *at least one* of the search terms is present. You are searching on the terms *college* and also *university* because documents containing either of these words might be relevant. Look at Figure 10.1.

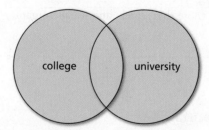

Figure 10.1 Using the term OR in a Boolean search.

The shaded circle with the word *college* represents all the records that contain the word *college*. The shaded circle with the word *university* represents all the records that contain the word *university*. The shaded overlap area represents all the records that contain both *college* and *university*.

OR logic is most commonly used to search for synonymous terms or concepts. The table on the next page is an example of how OR logic works.

OR logic collates the results to retrieve all the unique records containing one term, the other, or both. The more terms or concepts you combine in a search with OR logic, the more records you will retrieve.

SEARCH TERMS	RESULTS
college	1,220,000,000
university	1,440,000,000
college OR university	2,640,000,000

Using the term AND in a Boolean search

Goal: I'm interested in the relationship between poverty and crime.

Query: poverty AND crime

In this search, you retrieve records in which *both* of the search terms are present. This is illustrated in Figure 10.2 by the shaded area overlapping the two circles representing all the records that contain both the word *poverty* and the word *crime*.

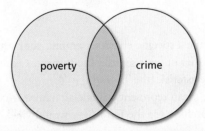

Figure 10.2 Using the term AND in a Boolean search.

Notice that we do not retrieve any records with only *poverty* or only *crime*. The corresponding table is an example of how AND logic works.

SEARCH TERMS	RESULTS
poverty	94,800,000
crime	518,000,000
poverty AND crime	4,600,000

The more terms or concepts we combine in a search with AND logic, the fewer records we will retrieve.

Using the term NOT in a Boolean search

Goal: I want information about cats, but I want to avoid anything about dogs.

Query: cats NOT dogs

In this search, we retrieve records in which *only one* of the terms is present. This is illustrated in Figure 10.3 by the shaded area with the word *cats* representing all the records containing the word *cats*.

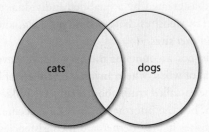

Figure 10.3 Using the term NOT in a Boolean search.

No records are retrieved in which the word *dogs* appears, even if the word *cats* appears there, too. The accompanying table shows how NOT logic works.

SEARCH TERMS	RESULTS
cats	317,000,000
dogs	399,000,000
cats NOT dogs	97,200,000

NOT logic excludes records from your search results. Be cautious when you use NOT: The term you *do* want may be present in an important way in documents that also contain the word you wish to avoid.

Wildcard Searches

In a wildcard search, you use a specific character among your search terms in a particular way to expand the boundaries of your search. The two most common characters used are the question mark and the asterisk (the "?" and the "*").

The question mark ("?") can represent a single alphanumeric character in a search expression. For example, searching for the term *ho?se* would yield results that contain such words as *house* and *horse*.

The asterisk ("*") can specify zero or more alphanumeric characters. It can be used in the middle or, more commonly, at the end of a word. Depending on where you place the asterisk, it can signify different words or just different forms of a single word.

For example, searching for the term *h*s* would yield results that contain such words as *his, homes, houses, horses, horticulturalists,* and *herbaceous.* Searching for the term *boat** would yield results such as *boats, boating,* and *boaters.* It is usually best to avoid using the asterisk as the first character in a search string.

A search term consisting of a lone asterisk and no other alphanumeric characters will retrieve every record from the database.

 # THE CREDIBILITY OF INFORMATION ONLINE

When you do online research, keep in mind that finding current, accurate information is better than finding lots of information. Just because something is posted online does not mean it is accurate and valid.

Do not take everything you find on the web at face value. Be critical of the websites you encounter in your research. Plagiarism is rampant on the web. Many times you can do a search and find numerous sites that contain exactly the same information. You can usually figure out on which site the information originated: the site set up the most professionally, listed as created by a qualified individual that cites references for the information. In general, websites that end in *.gov, .edu,* and *.org* tend to be more reliable than just *.com* and *.net* sites.

Beware of sites that do not account for their sources or have not been updated recently. Be especially critical of wikis, where anyone, regardless of knowledge or qualifications, can contribute to the so-called truth about a subject. Wikis can result in some very well-rounded information, but the information may be inaccurate. When qualified editors do not oversee a website, it may perpetuate inconsistencies, fallacies, and flat-out untruths about the topics discussed.

Even when information on the web seems accurate and professional, it can fool you. For example, if you search for the term *tree octopus* you will find images and associated websites. However, this is a hoax perpetuated online. There is no such animal—the sites, which seem real, are false, and the photos are manipulated. But only if you really read the results will you realize this. If you take those search results at face value and don't critically examine them, you will be fooled into believing there is such a creature as the fictional tree octopus.

Primary and Secondary Sources

The safest source for any information is the *primary source*, the place where the information was first expressed or put into print. In terms of technical research, a primary source is the study itself. If you are looking for information on music therapy, find a journal article describing an actual study on music therapy and the results. This would be your primary source.

Alternately, if you use a book, magazine, or Internet article that summarizes the findings of a number of music therapy research studies, you are using a *secondary source*, one that just restates information from its first occurrence. In general, the further you are from the primary source of information, the more likely there may be errors or oversights in the information.

The more often something is interpreted, the more chance there is of losing some meaning in translation. Never assume the first site to come up in search results is correct and adequate for your needs. Read through as many of the search results as you can. It will help you round out your perspective, as well as identify which sites stand out in terms of quality, readability, and scope of information. It will help you discover the fact that the tree octopus isn't real.

Try the search again using terms that are synonyms. This can be a way to fine-tune your results and maybe find information that is not as obvious.

Do your best to gain a well-rounded view of the information available. Try to find sites that come at the information from different angles.

You may find that after you look at several sites, you can see mistakes in some of them. But you only caught those mistakes because you looked at the big picture instead of just trying to take advantage of the fastest, easiest view.

ACADEMIC INTEGRITY AND PLAGIARISM

Doing research puts you in a position to present views relevant to your topic that are other than your own. You will discover many interesting ideas. But be sure you keep track of which ideas are your own and which come from other people. You must cite your sources correctly and give credit to others where it is due. That honesty in dealings regarding your coursework is known as academic integrity.

Plagiarism can be defined as "the unauthorized use or close imitation of the language and thoughts of another author and the representation of them as one's own original work" (*Dictionary.com Unabridged*; http://dictionary.reference.com/browse/plagiarism).

In other words, you are plagiarizing when you copy the words or the thoughts of someone else and do not tell your audience that those words or thoughts were not originally your own.

Looking Closely at Plagiarism

The most important point to consider about plagiarism is not just that it isn't fair to others or can result in serious consequences. It is that if you plagiarize, you are passing up a chance for learning.

What's Wrong with Plagiarizing?

If plagiarism becomes a tempting option, maybe you need to rethink your priorities. Have you given up on school? If not, then the reason you are here is to *learn*. Doing research, thinking through ideas, and articulating your thoughts in writing are all a big part of that learning experience. You forsake that part when you plagiarize.

There is much more to consider with regard to plagiarism, however. What may seem like an insignificant act can be taken as an indicator of various character traits. For any given instance of plagiarism, any of these might apply:

- *You are a thief.* You couldn't be bothered to put in the required amount of work in terms of the research, thought, and writing the assignment required. So you used someone else's thought, research, and work, and stole (from yourself!) the opportunity to learn.

- *You are unimaginative.* You used someone else's words and ideas, instead of paraphrasing or summarizing them so you couldn't, or didn't bother to, think of new ways to express the information and ideas.

- *You are dishonest.* You didn't cite the ideas or information that you used properly, so, in effect, you tried to pass them off as your own.

- *You are disrespectful.* You didn't have enough respect for those who conceived the original ideas or did important research on the topic to give them the credit they are due. In addition, you didn't have enough respect for the readers of your work to give them the facts of the situation.

- *You are unprofessional.* Being professional entails extending a certain level of courtesy to others and following the guidelines for a task, as well as acting ethically. By plagiarizing, you broadcast the fact that you do not care about professional standards and are neither courteous nor ethical. Is that the way you want to present yourself? Probably not. So take care not to plagiarize.

What If You Plagiarize Accidentally?

Maybe you didn't deliberately plagiarize; although it may have been an accident or an oversight, ignorance or accident is really no excuse. You will be informed of the proper ways to cite information for your assignments, but if you aren't, it is your responsibility to ask about it. Because plagiarism in itself is dishonest and sneaky, it can be difficult to give people who plagiarize the benefit of the doubt that it was not intentional.

Although the penalties for plagiarism vary widely by instructor and institution, it is always regarded as a serious offense. Students who plagiarize may be asked to redo the assignment. They may receive a failing grade for the assignment or for the course. They may be put on academic probation, or they may even be expelled.

Common Instances of Plagiarism

Plagiarism occurs when students include a small part of another person's work in their own without giving credit to the source or when students submit an entire paper or project created by another person. It can also occur when a whole paper is made up of small parts of others' work.

There are websites where students can purchase complete papers written on a wide variety of subjects for common courses. Your instructor knows that, too. There are also websites instructors can visit, and just by putting in a small excerpt of text and doing a search, they can find out if a student has misrepresented a part or the whole of the work put forward as his or her own.

In this Internet age, where information is so easy to obtain, it is just as easy to track. So if you ever consider plagiarizing, do not forget it is just as easy for an instructor to run a search on your work as it was for you to commit your crime. But we hope that as a person who values learning—an honest, imaginative, careful, respectful person, with a good work ethic—you will avoid plagiarizing.

Citing Sources

The way to avoid plagiarizing is to always cite your sources correctly. Citations are brief notes describing what information sources you used, who originally wrote them and when, and where you found them. They can take the form of footnotes, endnotes, notes within the text, or even a separate resource page that lists all the sources you referred to in your research.

Your school will probably determine which format you must use to cite your sources. Many colleges adopt style guides to be used in all courses that not only illustrate the citation style but also describe the specific page format and organization of papers. In other cases, the particular program, or the instructor, may determine the style guide/citation requirements.

In rare cases, you may find you are given no guidelines regarding what is expected for citing your sources. Seek guidance from the instructor. If none is forthcoming, decide yourself how you will present the citations. Pick a style and apply it, rather than just skipping mention of sources altogether. Always give credit where it is due.

Some common sources for document and citation styles are the *Publication Manual of the American Psychological Association*, the *Chicago Manual of Style*, and the *MLA Handbook for Writers of Research Papers*. Numerous style guides are available though, so rather than describing any specific style and formatting rules here, we advise you to find out what guide is required in your course or for your school. Many of the guides have associated websites that can be quite useful, so do not hesitate to do a search for information on your school's preferred guide.

MORE POWER ——————
TO YOU

Now is your chance to explore this chapter's topics further. Check out the sites listed here. Enjoy expanding your knowledge and *more power to you*!

Search Engines
www.thesearchenginelist.com/

Researching the Internet
www.studygs.net/research.htm

Thinking Like a Genius
www.studygs.net/genius.htm

Citing Websites
www.studygs.net/citation.htm

Thinking Critically
www.studygs.net/crtthk.htm

Wildcard Searches
http://apps.caes.uga.edu/impact/searchhelp.cfm

If any of these websites are not available or you wish to seek out additional information, we encourage you to do your own online search. Consider the concepts covered in the chapter that are most important to you, and think of various terms that could be used to describe them. For this chapter, some potential keywords to search include:

questioning techniques

critical thinking strategies

critical reading

online research

avoiding plagiarism

When searching online, consider different ways to express ideas. Remember to use synonyms and related words. Try phrasing things in different ways. And always review more than the first few pages of search results.

Strategies for Successful Online Learning

11

Power UP

- Monitor your own openness and ability to give and receive feedback. Your opportunity to learn from your instructor and peers is directly related to these qualities.

- Give feedback using appropriate guidelines.

- Be open and receptive to receiving feedback. Use it as a tool for self-improvement.

- Understand that online learning takes just as much time, if not more, than face-to-face learning. The difference is in the flexibility.

- Know how to listen online. Focus, limit extraneous noise, read closely, and pay attention to content and tone.

- Identify your own methods for effective note taking. Find the easiest way to gather and organize information so you can remember it.

- Recognize the importance of test preparation. Remember to study the material, have ready access to resources, and pace yourself as you take the exam.

A n open mind is a mind that can be educated. It is a given that you will want to open your mind to new concepts and perspectives in your online program. But you also want to open your mind when it comes to accepting and giving feedback.

FEEDBACK: GIVING IT AND ACCEPTING IT GRACEFULLY

Feedback is a necessary tool for helping anyone to improve, whether in an online or face-to-face environment. Accepting feedback may not always be easy. We all love positive feedback, but sometimes it is hard to swallow the negative feedback. Acknowledging and growing in our weak areas are how we can become more successful at anything.

Feedback does become a little trickier in the virtual environment. The lack of nonverbal communication signals makes it more difficult to understand a person's intentions. Without nonverbal cues, the giver of feedback has to concentrate on being succinct and careful with word choice.

We Love Feedback

For most online students, seeing feedback means the instructor is paying close attention to them and their online journey. Feedback can be taken as an indication that our work is of value. If you just spent several hours working on a major final paper, of course you want it to be read and appreciated.

Do remember, however, that many online classes today are not as teacher-centered as they were in the past. Teacher-centered feedback is based on the premise that the instructor lectures, with little interaction from the students except their occasional questions. Many classes today are focused less on the lecture itself and more on the experiences and opinions the students can add to enhance the lecture. Teachers are not only leaders but also skilled facilitators in the classroom. This approach to learning means you will have an opportunity to learn from your classmates as well as your instructor. In fact, even as instructors, we were always learning new things from our students. Your ability to learn from your instructor and your peers is directly related to your openness and ability to give and receive feedback.

Giving Feedback

To give feedback, you must be honest and constructive. "Go for the ball and not the player." Try to be tactful. If you can find something positive, say it, but if you can't, try to be as diplomatic as possible in your comments while still being constructive.

Here are some strategies to help you offer appropriate feedback in the online environment:

1. Be clear and succinct about what you want to say. Reread your message before you send it for clarity, punctuation, and grammar. The more error-free your message, the easier it will be to understand its intent. The more concise you are with your written communication, the less chance there will be of misinterpreting the goal of the feedback.

2. Emphasize the positive aspects of the feedback in the opening of your message, and always end the message with a positive and motivating tone. In the body of the message, provide the feedback and any constructive criticism you think is necessary.

3. Be descriptive in your feedback, rather than evaluative or judgmental.

4. Do not make any generalizations or assumptions when giving feedback; avoid words like *all*, *never*, *always*, *everyone*, *only*, and *you*.

5. Limit your advice on how to fix the work. Often the most useful feedback is helping the person to recognize or better understand the area(s) that need improvement.

Receiving Feedback

As a receiver of feedback in the online environment, be aware of the restrictions on the person giving the feedback. Try not to make any assumptions, and go only by what is clearly stated. View the feedback with the understanding that whether it is positive or negative, feedback is meant to be constructive, not derogatory. Keep an open mind and try your best not to be defensive.

Feedback is a tool to help you improve, not an insult. Look at it as a quality improvement process. If you already knew everything, there would be no reason for you to be in school. You are in class to learn, and receiving feedback is part of that process. Here are some tips for focusing on the helpful messages in the feedback:

1. Divorce yourself from your emotions and try just to hear the criticism. Do not make excuses or evaluate whether it is right or wrong. Just listen.

2. Look for the practical advice within the feedback. *Yadda, yadda, nice job on this but what you can do to improve is X, yadda yadda.* Pick out the really constructive part of the message that you need to keep in mind for the future.

3. If the feedback was mostly criticism without any constructive advice, and you really do not know how to address the issue, go back to the person who gave it. If that is not an option, find someone else who would understand. Try to discover what steps you might reasonably take to make an improvement.

4. Try to see the big picture. Have you gotten feedback with similar comments before? Are there common areas that people always bring up? Clue in, and realize that if you are hearing it often or from multiple sources, the chances are it is accurate. Do something about it.

5. Realize that people who give you feedback often have your best interests at heart.

One of your authors recalls receiving a paper back from an instructor that puzzled her: He gave her an A, but he also wrote a few notes on how she could have made the paper better. She was confused. If it was an A paper, then why all the criticism and advice on how to improve it? She asked him about it, and he told her that although it was an excellent paper, it was not perfect. There is always room for improvement, and he thought she could do an even better job next time. She never looked at feedback the same way again.

Part of the reason you are taking classes is to better yourself. So be open and receptive to feedback, and use it as a tool for self-improvement.

KEEPING TIME IN MIND

One of the largest misconceptions about online learning revolves around time. Many people who have never taken an online class make the assumption that online learning takes less time than learning in a traditional classroom.

In truth, as we said before, online learning takes just as much, if not more, time. The difference comes in the flexibility of your time.

Because time is such an important variable in the online environment, we next discuss some tactics that relate to time management in the virtual classroom.

Time on Task

Keep in mind that if you were in an on-ground class, you would probably spend about 3 hours per credit per week. Thus you would be expected to spend roughly 9 hours per week reading, studying, and completing assignments. This expectation applies to both online and face-to-face classes. The exact amount of time will vary depending on you and on the particular course.

Because of the flexibility in an online class, people may get carried away in either direction, dedicating too much or too little time to a course. Remember that the point of the course is not for you to post the most messages to the class. Neither is it for you to squeak through by doing as little as possible. If you want to succeed and actually learn in class, you need to put in the effort.

As you gain more experience in online learning, you will figure out how much time you need to spend to do well. If you pay attention and pace yourself, you will learn what it takes to meet your desired goals.

Every class may be a little different in the amount of time you allot for your studies. Much of this will depend on your previous base of knowledge regarding the curriculum and how quickly you are able to catch on, retain, and apply the information you need from the class.

Pacing Yourself

There are two basic and very different ways to approach how you will spend your time in the online classroom. The first is not to worry about exactly how much time you are spending on each item in advance. Jump into each topic with an open mind, and simply spend as much time as you need to absorb the information. This approach is ideal for students who do not have large time restrictions.

However, the majority of students, especially those who have chosen to take online classes, generally have time constraints. The second method is to develop formulas for how much time you are willing to commit to various aspects of the class.

For instance, a common formula might be to look at the time you want to spend on an assignment and correlate it directly to how many points the assignment is worth. Is a 5-point paper really worth 20 hours of your time?

For some people, it is easy to drown in a project, spending an inordinate amount of time (say 20 hours) on a project that is only worth 5 points out of a class total of 100 points. Consider that it might be logical to put the most time into the projects worth the most points. The assumption, after all, is that those projects that are worth more will take more time and research and thought than the ones that are not worth as much.

In contrast, there are other people who start a project and then immediately become frustrated with it before spending any major amount of time or making any progress. These people tend to radically overestimate the amount of time they spend. Before you give up on something, or decide it is not worth more of your time, estimate realistically the time you have actually put into it.

Consider how much time it takes you to do something and how much time a project actually warrants. For instance, when one of your authors was in her online program, she created a formula for how much time to spend on homework. It went something like this: 5 hours = a paper worth 10% of my grade and 10 hours = a paper worth 20% of my grade.

She used that formula as a guideline to make sure she was not spending too much or too little time on an assignment. You will have to work out your own formula if you are a person who likes that approach. But even if you do not use a formula, assigning a reasonable amount of time to spend on a project is a good idea.

One final thought: The work does not have to be perfect—it just has to meet the instructor's requirements. Sometimes it won't matter if you spend 100 hours on the paper; it is not going to get any better than it was after 5 hours . . . it just won't. It is good enough. It met the requirements in the syllabus, you learned what you needed to learn, so be done with it and move on to something else. Too often people freeze and do not get it finished because of not having the ability to let go.

STUDY SKILLS

The basic skills that will help you be a successful student in an online course are the same as those in an on-ground course: paying attention, taking notes, and studying for tests. However, you might want to consider them from a slightly different angle in this new environment.

Paying Attention

You need to be focused when you are reading in the classroom, so you fully grasp all levels of the message. Being fully focused means the following:

- Not trying to multitask while reading the message.

- Making sure noises around you are not interfering with your concentration, like television or other people trying to talk to you.

- Not rushing through because you are tired or you have time constraints. The flexibility of the online environment that allows you to attend class at any time is a great thing. But it is your responsibility to realize that if you are dozing off while working on a paper at 1 in the morning, maybe you are not doing right by the assignment or yourself.

If you are reading a message, it is essential for you to know what the sender of the message is saying (content), how he or she is saying it (tone), and finally the motive behind the message (intent). Rephrase messages that are unclear and pose them back to the sender as questions (e.g., "So, what I hear you saying is _____; is that correct?") to be sure you understand the message.

Without knowing the meaning of a message, you cannot respond to the message accurately and appropriately. Keep in mind, if you were in an on-ground class, you would not have a lot of noise around you. You would be dedicating your time in class to focusing on the content, your instructor, and fellow students.

Taking Notes

Do you need to take notes online? The answer really depends on you. Do not feel you have to take notes a certain way, because the most effective way for you to take notes (if any) is through your own note-taking preference.

Everyone has a personal learning style. Applying your learning style can help you process information more effectively. The most effective note-taking method for you will depend on your learning style. Listed here are some different techniques. Consider trying some or all of them to see what works best for you:

- Print out course content. Make notes in the margin or highlight pertinent sections.

- Copy and paste relevant sections of reading or lecture into a new document.

- Rewrite important information in your own language.

- Summarize the main ideas from the content (see Figure 11.1a).
- Use a fishbone diagram to denote cause and effect (see Figure 11.1b).
- Use mind mapping to make connections visually (see Figure 11.1c).

Effective note taking means finding the easiest way to gather and organize the information so you can remember it.

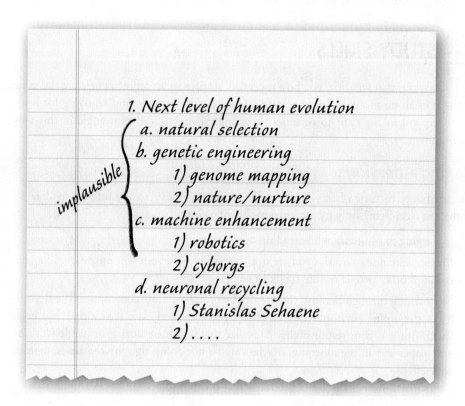

1. Next level of human evolution
 a. natural selection
 b. genetic engineering
   1) genome mapping
   2) nature/nurture
 c. machine enhancement
   1) robotics
   2) cyborgs
 d. neuronal recycling
   1) Stanislas Sehaene
   2) . . . .

implausible

Figure 11.1a Examples of Different Note-Taking Strategies: *Summarizing the Main Ideas.*

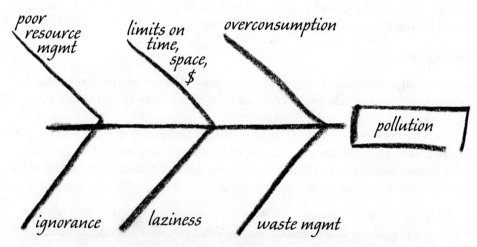

poor resource mgmt

limits on time, space, $

overconsumption

pollution

ignorance

laziness

waste mgmt

Figure 11.1b Examples of Different Note-Taking Strategies: *Fishbone Diagram*

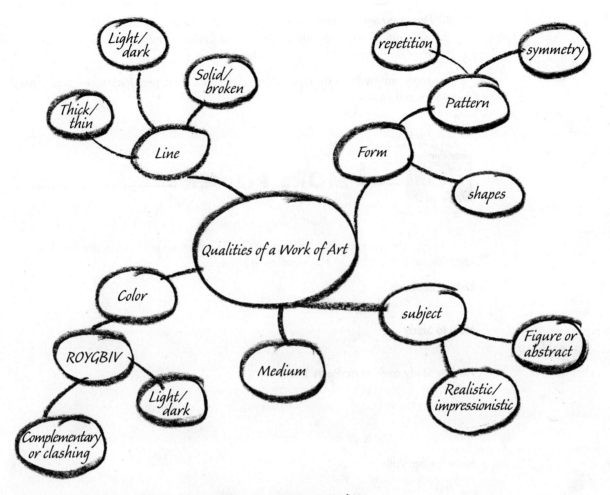

Figure 11.1c Examples of Different Note-Taking Strategies: *A Mind Map*

Testing in the Online Environment

You may not take very many tests online; in fact, you may not take any. Depending on your course/program, you may not be assessed through tests but only through alternative types of assignments like papers and projects. If you do have to take a test in an online course, it will likely be an open-book exam or you may have to do it in a proctored environment.

Regardless of the type of test you are taking, you need to study the same way you would for an on-ground class test. That is, *you need to know the material.* Many students fail an online test, even if it is open book, because they do not plan properly. There are three principles we recommend:

1. ***Prepare.*** Take the time to study before the test and have all your resources immediately available within reach when you actually take the test. Do what you can to increase your efficiency, such as tabbing the chapter summaries and having all your notes organized by topic.

2. ***Take advantage of the resources available to you as an online student.*** Know what tools and resources are available and allowed for you to use when you take the test. Be resourceful in the online environment. Be aware that when the instructors designed these tests, they knew you would have access to a multitude of resources. They factored that into the design of their assessment, so do not expect that just because an online test is open book it will be easy.

3. *Pace yourself.*   Know how much time you have to spend on the test. In some cases, online tests are only available for a limited window of time, so be ready to focus on it completely when you choose to start.

For more information on note-taking methods or test preparation, we recommend you do a search online.

MORE POWER TO YOU

Now is your chance to explore this chapter's topics further. Check out the sites listed here. Enjoy expanding your knowledge and *more power to you*!

Using Feedback
www.studygs.net/feedback.htm

How to Study
www.howtostudy.org

How to Study and Learn: Parts 1–4
www.criticalthinking.org/articles/sts-ct-teaching-students-study-learn-p1.cfm
www.criticalthinking.org/articles/sts-ct-teaching-students-study-learn-p2.cfm
www.criticalthinking.org/articles/sts-ct-teaching-students-study-learn-p3.cfm
www.criticalthinking.org/articles/sts-ct-teaching-students-study-learn-p4.cfm

Note-Taking Skills
www.arc.sbc.edu/notes.html

Note-Taking Methods
www.alextech.edu/en/CollegeServices/SupportServices/StudySkills/LectureNoteTaking/MethodsOfNoteTaking.aspx

Study Skills Help Information
www.ucc.vt.edu/stdysk/stdyhlp.html

If any of these websites are not available or you wish to seek out additional information, we encourage you to do your own online search. Consider the concepts covered in the chapter that are most important to you, and think of various terms that could be used to describe them. For this chapter, some potential keywords to search include:

giving receiving feedback

online student study tips

note taking strategies

test taking

When searching online, consider different ways to express ideas. Remember to use synonyms and related words. Try phrasing things in different ways. And always review more than the first few pages of search results.

For more specific information on searching online, refer to Chapter 10.

The Evolution of Learning

12

Power UP

- Understand what is expected of you, and what you can expect, in today's world of higher education.

- Practice the real skills that will make you successful in the classroom and beyond.

- Be aware of some of the less common tools and technologies being used to support learning.

EVOLVING LEARNERS

Somewhere, over their rainbow, is "a vision for student success in the new global economy." These are the words of the Partnership for 21st Century Skills, a cooperative effort focused on identifying and developing educational strategies to serve 21st-century students. The 21st century is now. *You* are a 21st-century student. But what does this mean?

Already into the second decade of the millennium, we have seen the transformational power of the Information Age. Students today play with toys whose technology is more sophisticated than what was available to early astronauts. What will the world be like for students in 5 years? In 10? In 20? What skills will be demanded of "digital natives" to navigate work/life in the 21st century? Being born into technology is in itself no guarantee of success. What will be required to prepare *you* for a world that grows progressively smaller and flatter? "Why smaller and flatter," you ask? A world that is smaller and flatter simply means that we can more easily see and communicate with others across the globe via technology.

21ST-CENTURY SKILLS

A model that communicates crucial 21st-century skills, and their tie-in to education, has been offered by the Partnership for 21st Century Skills (P21). As illustrated in Figure 12.1, these skills fall into three groups: Learning and Innovation; Information, Media, and Technology; and Life and Career. Let's talk a little more about exactly how these skills apply to you.

Learning and Innovation Skills

These skills include originality, inventiveness, and adaptability, as well as the ability to think critically, solve problems creatively, and learn quickly. These skills and abilities will be essential in the workplace of the future and a world where life is characterized by

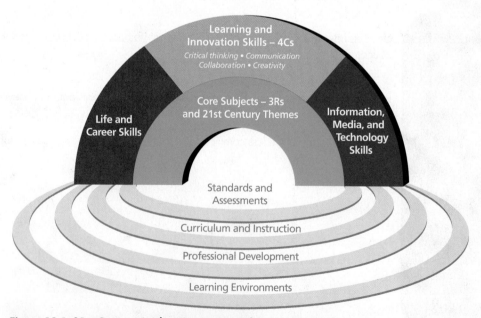

Figure 12.1 21st-Century Student Outcomes and Support Systems

Source: © 2010 Partnership for 21st Century Skills (P21), www.p21.org. Used with permission.

change and complexity. You probably already practice some of these skills on a daily basis, but you should think about how you can sharpen the skills you already have as well as develop new ones.

Not only is the workplace becoming increasingly virtual, it is also being populated by work groups that are scattered regionally, nationally, or globally. Effective communication and collaboration have always been valuable skills—among innovative and multicultural knowledge workers, they are especially important. These are key survival skills for those of us who live under conditions that continually shift in response to events that might be occurring half a world away. P21 stresses flexibility in diverse viewpoints, as well as synthesizing feedback. (You might recognize these are subjects we have discussed in previous chapters.)

Information, Media, and Technology Skills

In a world that is already technology and media rich, it is easy to see how skills in these areas hold the key to future success. Learners will need to achieve both information and media literacy. Information literacy, according to the American Library Association:

> . . . forms the basis for lifelong learning. It is common to all disciplines, to all learning environments, and to all levels of education. It enables learners to master content and extend their investigations, become more self-directed, and assume greater control over their own learning. An information literate individual is able to:

1. Determine the extent of information needed
2. Access the needed information effectively and efficiently
3. Evaluate information and its sources critically
4. Incorporate selected information into one's knowledge base
5. Use information effectively to accomplish a specific purpose
6. Understand the economic, legal, and social issues surrounding the use of information, and access and use information ethically and legally.

Certain actions on that list are easier to accomplish than others. As an online learner, numbers 2, 4, and 5 probably come naturally to you, but we suggest that everyone can use practice in numbers 1, 3, and 6.

Media literacy is a complement to information literacy. By media literacy, we mean the ability to communicate competently in all media forms as well as to access, understand, analyze, evaluate, and participate with the powerful images, words, and sounds that make up our contemporary mass media culture. Again, these are probably skills that you mostly possess already. Not surprisingly, these are skills that will be necessary in school and on the job.

An easy way to conceptualize the ideas of information and media literacy is simply to think of them as input and output. Information literacy is about the way we bring information into our brains—search, find, and discriminate good from bad—and media literacy is about the way we present that information to others—the tools we use, as well as the skill we show in using them.

Life and Career Skills

Harnessing technology and managing information will not be enough to succeed in the decades to come. Mastery of 21st-century technology must be accompanied by such personal qualities as initiative and self-direction, social and cross-cultural awareness, responsibility, and leadership. Throughout school and into adulthood, these skills will be essential in a global economy.

How can you achieve these 21st-century skills and be prepared to be successful in jobs that don't yet exist? Our advice to you is to be honest about your skills and abilities, be willing to learn, and be aware of the ways in which *you* learn best. The good news is that there are lots of resources and options available regarding the ways in which you can learn.

Evolving Technology for Learning

Regardless of the ways in which you learn best, engagement is an essential element in learning for everyone. Most of us become easily and completely immersed in activities that foster interactivity, control, challenge, and excitement—even when a task is difficult and success is not guaranteed. More than ever before, this kind of learning takes place in multiplayer online role-playing games, on simulated worlds enabled by devices like smartphones, iPads, and portable readers. In these technology-dependent virtual environments, students practice "real world" skills through virtual experiences. Individually and collectively, students of today connect, discuss, create, reason, critique, solve problems, evaluate, and make decisions—skills that form the foundation of 21st-century success.

Let's look at some real-life scenarios where technology is taking learning to a new level:

- American students learning Chinese can teleconference in real time with Chinese students who are learning English.

- Instead of producing static hard-copy reports, middle schoolers can post their compositions on their web page and obtain comments and critiques from visitors.

- Students can demonstrate their mastery of technology, as well as subject matter, by producing websites, videos, video games, and music.

The latest technology and emerging devices are taking learning to a new level.

Gaming

"Serious games" are a boon to education. Using video game technology, serious games capitalize on the power of video games to "attract, engage, connect, and teach gameplayers critical content in the games respective focus area" (Annetta et al., 2006, p. 16).

Serious games engage learners of all ages and provide opportunities to encourage active and critical learning. They allow learners to take risks in a virtual space where real-world negative consequences, such as grading or embarrassment, are lessened. These games provide rewards that are customized to individual ability levels, effort, and mastery. The game environment affords practice in a context that mirrors reality, but without real consequences.

Will Wright, the inventor of *The Sims* and *Spore*, said "players learn through failure, which is the best route to excellence" (http://fora.tv/2009/04/02/Will_Wright_on_Spore_Simcity_and_The-Sims). Wright alluded to a study involving two pottery classes, one in which students had to spend a session making the best possible single pot and the other in which students were told to make as many pots as possible in the same time span. The second approach produced the most high-quality pots.

Chances are good that there will be an opportunity for you to play a serious game in one of your classes if you are taking a learning program that is entirely online. It really does depend on your institution and/or your faculty member, though, and the way in which they like to conduct their classes. You may want to ask your instructor if there is an opportunity to have a serious game tied to your learning.

Remember though, that the bigger production games that you may normally think of as serious games are not always possible in the classroom for several reasons:

- The huge amount of resources needed and high cost to create those games
- The fact that more elaborate games take a great deal of time to play
- The difficulty of linking truly dynamic, complex virtual situations to static learning objectives

There are a slew of "casual games" that cost a lot less to produce. While not necessarily as engaging and "serious" for learners, these simpler games still give you the opportunity to play and practice at the same time. These are the ones that you are more likely to see in your online courses. Some examples are puzzle games such as crosswords, matching games, physics-based games like bowling, trivia games, and more.

Simulations

Webster's Dictionary defines a simulation as "the imitation of some real thing, state of affairs, or process." So, let's translate that into learning. The power of 21st-century technology enables us to overcome learning barriers that are often associated with online learning. In the past you might have heard people say:

"You can't possibly take a speech class online."

"There is no way you can have an application course/clinical type of course online."

"You really think you can talk online in groups?"

Through simulations, you *can* take a speech class online. There *is* a way to conduct application/clinical type exercises online. And we all know by now that you can talk in groups online—in chat rooms.

Through the formation of learning networks that link peers, subject matter experts, and various institutions, we can all experience a level of authentic learning that was never before possible. Content can be delivered in numerous interactive ways, including the use of virtual worlds. In virtual worlds you can experience and explore any country, any planet, and any time period throughout history. If you are asked to go on a "virtual field trip" in your class, you are in luck, because you are about to enter a unique, cost-effective, and exciting new way to learn about new things, events, processes, and places. For example, Indiana University of Pennsylvania took a virtual field trip to a dig that was created for archaeology students.

Second Life is probably the most well-known virtual world environment. In this 3-D virtual world, users can socialize, customize an avatar (an *avatar* is a computer user's representation of himself/herself or alter ego usually in the form of a 3-D model used in computer games), and connect and learn using voice and text.

Mobile Devices in Learning

In the same way that new applications, such as games and simulations, are changing the landscape of education, new tools are revolutionizing student access to content. Smartphones and e-book readers are among the mobile devices that are broadening and changing access to education.

Mobile Learning, as it relates to e-learning, refers to learning through the use of devices that can be easily carried. Some of these devices include:

- Apple iPod Touch
- Apple iPad
- Apple iPhone
- Android-powered Smartphones
- Android-powered Tablets

Mobile solutions enable teachers to provide ongoing feedback, inconspicuously, to students and parents. Just like in the online classroom via a computer, a student is able to learn individually, in groups, and peer-to-peer via mobile learning.

Mobile learning is *not a requirement* when you take an online class, though depending on the curriculum you may be able to choose to use mobile devices to assist you in your online learning journey. Why might you consider having a mobile learning device to complement your online learning experience?

- Quick access to required resources if you are not near a computer
- Easily maintained wireless connectivity
- The ability to study with familiar tools you already use regularly
- The convenience of downloading lectures and other audio to Smartphones for use at your leisure

Unlike cell phones and PDAs, whose primary purpose is communication, an e-book reader is an electronic device that is designed primarily for the purpose of entertainment, but the line is blurring into education. Tablet computers such as readers are intended for reading digital books and periodicals. Some of these devices include:

- Amazon Kindle
- Barnes & Noble Nook
- Apple iPad

As mentioned above, mobile learning is not a requirement when you take an online class, though you might *choose* to use an e-reader to assist you in your online class. Why might you think about using an e-reader?

- Using a portable e-book reader means that you don't have to lug those heavy piles of books with you.
- Purchasing digital textbooks for use on an e-book device can save you a significant amount of money over hardcover books.
- e-book readers are environmentally friendly.

Many people believe that eventually all computing will be mobile, which means that all learning will be mobile. Regardless, it's important to understand that 21st-century learning makes the most of various types of classrooms, immersive and interactive learning environments, and associated devices. Their use and applications are limited only by the creativity of educators and instructional designers. Students, too, can be counted on for input into how they are used in the future. What an exciting time to be an online learner!

MORE POWER
TO YOU

Now is your chance to explore this chapter's topics further. Check out the sites listed here. Enjoy expanding your knowledge and *more power to you!*

All About Smartphones
www.apple.com/iphone/
www.motorola.com/Consumers/US-EN/Consumer-Product-and-Services/Mobile-Phones/
Motorola-DROID-US-EN

Everything a Tablet Should Be
www.apple.com/ipad/
www.motorola.com/Consumers/US-EN/Consumer-Product-and-Services/Tablets

Understanding Specific Examples of Simulations
http://phet.colorado.edu/
http://secondlife.com/whatis/

If any of these websites are not available or you wish to seek out additional information, we encourage you to do your own online search. Consider the concepts covered in the chapter that are most important to you, and think of various terms that could be used to describe them. For this chapter, some potential keywords to search include:

m-learning

21st century skills+online learning

learning games

educational simulations

When searching online, consider different ways to express ideas. Remember to use synonyms and related words. Try phrasing things in different ways. And always review more than the first few pages of search results.

For more specific information on searching online, refer to Chapter 10.

Computer
Concerns

13

Power UP

Recognize your computer as the primary tool you will use in the online environment. Make sure both the hardware and software are set up for ease of use.

Be aware of how to work with documents on the computer. Familiarize yourself with the capabilities of the main computer programs.

Know the options available within your e-mail program for organizing and sending messages.

Computer skills are a necessity in this day and age. In fact, it is doubtful that the younger generations in elementary school today will ever have to upgrade their computer skills. Computers are a part of our everyday life and have changed the culture in which we live in many ways.

Your computer is the primary tool you will use in the online environment. It provides not only your access to the course, but also all the other tools that will enable you to communicate with people in the online environment and complete your assignments. Thus, you must have at least a rudimentary understanding of the main parts and programs of your computer and how to use them.

You may already know most of the information in this chapter. But if you are unfamiliar with these terms and concepts, you may find it helpful to do additional research on your own to fully develop your knowledge and technical expertise. Refining your computer skills will pay off in the long run.

COMPUTER ISSUES

Probably your most important tools as an online student are the right computer and hardware. This hardware should include a monitor, keyboard, mouse/touch pad, and memory.

Some of you may already have a computer, but for those who do not, choosing a computer can be complicated. First, calculate your budget. Then decide what you are going to do with the computer. If you are going to check e-mail, surf the web, and write letters, in addition to taking your online class, you want a different configuration than if you are going to play games or manipulate photos. We assume here that you are probably looking for the activities listed in the first example. You should also know that, just like when you buy a car, almost as soon as you purchase a machine it becomes outdated. Bigger, better, newer, and faster happens about every 6 months in the world of computers!

Many hardware options are available to you.

Hardware

Hardware is the term used to describe the parts of your computer that are tangible and take up space on your desk or in the machine.

The *monitor* is the screen on which the computer projects images of your computer desktop or different software programs such as Word or Excel or web pages. Look at a series of monitors. What size monitor do you really need to take an online class? Make sure the monitor is bright enough for you to see. The monitor should be comfortable for *your* eyes, not the salesperson's. Currently, inexpensive monitors provide adequate resolutions for everyday use. Don't be distracted by the case or the color of the frame. Look at the screen. Look at a few different pictures. If they all look good to you, choose the one with the lowest price.

The *keyboard* contains the alphabetic, numeric, and other buttons you use to type messages and documents. There are different types of keyboards, such as standard, ergonomic, and portable. There are even flexible and glow-in-the-dark keyboards. Find a keyboard that suits your needs.

Keep in mind that keyboards also vary in the action of the keys—how hard or how easy it is to press them down—so make that a consideration for your choice as well.

The *mouse* or *touch pad* is the tool you use to move the cursor on the screen and select or "click" on certain areas. A mouse is a separate piece from your machine. It may be linked to the computer by a cord or it may be wireless. A touch pad performs the same actions as a mouse, but it is integrated into the keyboard of the computer or laptop. Currently, an optical mouse is the easiest to use. It does not have a roller ball to get dirty. Do not buy a touch pad until you try it out. Make sure you know how to adjust its response levels. Choose the keyboard, mouse, and touch pad according to your personal comfort and taste.

The *memory* is the part of your computer that retains information for future retrieval. In general, the computer itself should have at least 1 gig of memory and a video card that supports the monitor you choose. You cannot see the memory of your computer. It is buried inside the machine, and it is probably not a part you will handle much yourself. We need to mention it, though, because you do not want to run out of memory. The memory on your machine can become full depending on these factors:

- How much memory your machine has
- How much information you tend to save
- How often you clean out your mailbox and how often you eliminate extraneous information, like browser cookies, temp files, and your computer's virtual trash basket

If you buy a fast central processing unit (CPU) and a large amount of memory, the machine will probably keep you satisfied for 5 or 6 years. If you do not know how to empty your trash, delete your cookies or temp files, or clean out your mailbox, research these topics online or ask a computer-savvy friend to help you.

Even if you do know how to eliminate obsolete or extraneous information from your machine, you may find that in time, as you do more work and save it for future reference, the memory of your machine fills to near capacity. If you let it fill up, you will not be able to save anything new. So try to keep track of how much space you have left in memory, and when the free space becomes slim, consider adding memory to your machine. A computer store or tech-savvy friend can help you with this. As technology continues to improve, more memory becomes available in smaller packages at lower prices.

Operating Systems

To run other programs, a computer must have an operating system, which comes in many different forms. They all control the CPU and its devices. However, because CPUs are not all the same, they must be talked to differently. An operating system (OS) acts like a bridge between the user and the CPU.

When it comes to computers, the Windows OS created by Microsoft is probably the most common one used today. Close behind Windows is Macintosh. Many people have strong preferences regarding one OS or another. When it comes to smartphones, the common OSs are Apple and Google/Android.

The important thing for you to know is which one(s) are allowed in your online program. Some programs are open to both of these systems. Some only allow Windows users. Before you purchase a new machine or sign on to an online program, make sure you find out the OS requirements for the school's online program.

Common Software Programs

The software for a computer is just another layer between the user and the operating system. Simply put, a computer program is a set of instructions that tells a computer what to do. Next we describe some of the more common software programs you will likely be using in your classes.

Word-Processing Software

Microsoft Word (www.office.microsoft.com)

Corel WordPerfect (http://corel.com)

Both Word and WordPerfect are word-processing programs. They are designed to create documents by combining a comprehensive set of writing tools with an easy-to-use interface. Whenever you write a paper, or take notes, or put together a simple table, you will probably be using one of these word-processing programs.

Presentation Software

Microsoft PowerPoint (http://office.microsoft.com/en-us/powerpoint/default.aspx)

Prezi (http://prezi.com/)

PowerPoint is presentation software. Using this program, you can create dynamic and high-impact presentations using text, images, and even animations arranged on slides. Although you are taking your classes online, you still may be required to create presentations, so you will probably need to become familiar with this program.

Another program you can use to create presentations, if permissible for use in your class, is Prezi. Prezi is a more graphic-oriented way of staging your presentation, which can sometimes hold people's attention better than PowerPoint. If you are unfamiliar with Prezi, you can visit the website listed to see sample presentations and download the free version of the program.

Spreadsheet Software

Microsoft Excel (http://office.microsoft.com/en-us/excel/default.aspx)

Excel is a spreadsheet program. It sets up data as worksheets and workbooks, similar to an accounting ledger. You can use formulas within Excel to perform mathematical operations on the data. Excel lets you arrange data into rows, columns, and tables to manage, share, and analyze the information.

A multitude of other software programs are available for such activities as playing or composing music; creating web pages, diagrams, and art; and for many other functions. But these three types of programs are the main ones you will use as an online student. For each of them, you can easily discover a variety of online tutorials simply by doing a web search.

Internet Connections

In addition to the proper interface and software, another necessity for taking part in online learning is an Internet connection. Your course will be posted somewhere on the World Wide Web, and the web will also probably be your main resource for research and information. To connect to the web, you will need one of the types of connections shown in Table 13.1.

In addition to the types included in Table 13.1, there are also two other categories of connection: LAN (local area connection) and wireless (wireless router). You might have a T1 LAN connection at work and wireless cable access at home.

As you can see, there tends to be a direct correlation between the cost of the connection and the speed it offers. The speed, or bits per second, of an online connection is the main factor in how long it will take you to download or upload information from the Internet. If you have a fast connection, loading can happen almost instantaneously.

Table 13.1 Types of Internet Connections		
TYPE OF CONNECTION	**SPEED**	**COST**
Phone line (dial-up)	~ 56 kb/sec	Varies, but usually lowest
DSL (T1 or T3)	~ 1–3 mb/sec	Varies, but higher than dial-up
Cable	~ 5–10 mb/sec	Varies, but higher than dial-up
3G/4G (wireless)	~ 100 mb/sec	Varies, but usually highest of all

If you have a slow connection, uploads and downloads can be tedious and sometimes incomplete.

You may want to shop around for the right connection package for your needs. Cost can be affected by the competition among your local Internet service providers. Speed can be affected not only by your connection type, but also by the reliability of your service provider, how many other people are using your same connection (e.g., on a LAN), or by how many people are accessing a particular site at the same time. The time of day can impact the latter two factors.

You may opt for a dial-up connection, or not have a choice in the matter. The lower cost of a dial-up connection is paid for in the slower speed for downloads. That time could be saved with a digital subscriber line (DSL) or a faster moving Internet connection. This may not be an option for everyone, but if you can manage it, it is preferable.

Besides price and speed, connections can vary in accessibility and reliability. Certain types of connections may not be available in the area where you live. Depending on the newness and robustness of the connection materials, some connection types may be more reliable than others. One of your authors once had a dial-up connection that ran through underground phone lines which would often experience static during and after a rainstorm. The static meant she was frequently disconnected from the Internet whenever the ground was wet. Weather can be a major factor in the quality of your connection. High wind, lightning, and rain can all impact your connection, so be aware and try to plan ahead if possible.

WORKING WITH COMPUTER DOCUMENTS

As an online learner, most of the assignments you complete will be in the form of documents. You will spend a lot of time creating, editing, and uploading documents on the computer. There are a few tasks with which you should be familiar.

Creating, Formatting, and Saving Documents

The three most basic actions you will need to be proficient at are creating a new document, setting up the document, and saving it for future reference.

Creating Documents

When you first open any word-processing program, it offers you a new blank page on which to start writing. Most programs have a "button" on the menu at the top of the page you can select to start another new document (in Word, it is a small white rectangle, a blank page).

How you start off any new document is up to you. You will need to determine whether it is with an outline, or freewriting, or a series of notes. Once you start any document, it is a good idea to insert page numbers.

Formatting Documents

Formatting refers to how you set up the document and organize the information it contains. It can cover everything from paper size and margins to the fonts used in the headings and body of a document. The description of any assignment should specify the formatting requirements. Pay attention to these requirements. Sometimes you can miss enough points to fail the assignment when you do not format a paper correctly.

Knowing how to use the formatting options will pay off when your papers look professional and meet formatting requirements. You need to know how to do the following:

- Set margins
- Select the font size and type
- Italicize, bold, and underline text
- Add page numbers
- Insert headers and footers
- Cut/copy and paste within a document and from one document to another
- Use bullets and numbering
- Create tables
- Insert page and section breaks
- Create a new folder
- Save a document

Options for these actions are available through buttons or menus within the program.

If you are not familiar with how to perform any of these functions, take the time to learn. Explore the program on your own, or use the Help or Assistant options that are provided. You might ask for some basic document formatting lessons from a computer-savvy friend or find an online tutorial. You can also purchase one of the many guides to common software programs carried by bookstores or the local library. Becoming proficient in using your software will help you succeed in the online classroom.

Saving Documents

Saving documents is simple, right? You just click on that little icon, right? Well, there is more to all of this than that, so let us explain!

You need to learn not only *how* to save a document but to also consider the *what*, *where*, and *when* of file management. So, *what* do you want to save? We suggest you save everything you are working on. You can always delete it later. But you want the option to easily reference past work—whether it is notes, freewriting, or assignments—during all of your classes and even beyond your educational program.

Where you save your documents is key. Set up virtual folders on your computer that are well-organized. Categorize items logically. Create a well thought-out framework of folders that will make it simpler to locate saved documents later on. And make sure you save these documents with relevant file names, so when you go back to find them you know exactly what the material is, as well as the version. Many times instructors will dictate how a file must be named in order to submit an assignment for class. Pay attention to the information required, and make sure you organize things in such a way that, for any assignment, you are able to distinguish both your draft and final documents.

Now the *when*, which leads us to the most important rule when it comes to saving documents: Save often! We talk more about emergency backup in the final chapter of this book, but for now, keep in mind that computers are sensitive machines. You never know what might cause a document to be lost—power outages, power surges, viruses, hardware failure, to name just a few catastrophes! You increase your chances of keeping a document for posterity if you continuously save while you work. Don't wait until you have written every word of your 500–700 word paper to hit that save button. Save documents periodically as you work on them, *especially* after you make any major modifications.

Saving all your work continuously, and developing a logical system for naming files and folders, will prevent headaches later on.

WORKING WITH E-MAIL

Not only do you need to master your word-processing program, you also need to be skillful in handling e-mail.

Here are some of the actions that we recommend you know:

- Adjusting the font size, color, and type of messages
- Attaching documents to e-mail messages
- Using CC (courtesy copy) and BCC (blind courtesy copy)
- Setting up preferences in your system for such options as the spell-checker and the format of replies
- Creating a signature line

The same advice applies to learning all these tasks as to creating documents. Explore the program on your own, or use the Help or Assistant options provided. Ask for some basic e-mail formatting lessons from a computer-savvy friend. Find an online tutorial. Purchase one of the many guides to common software programs sold at bookstores, or check it out from your local library.

Becoming proficient at all these skills is in your own best interest. Do not forget to review the guidelines for online communication techniques in Chapter 8.

 MORE POWER TO YOU

Now is your chance to explore this chapter's topics further. Check out the sites listed here. Enjoy expanding your knowledge and *more power to you*!

Outline of Computer Literacy Skills
www.mcps.k12.md.us/departments/techlit/docs/Levels%20of%20Use.pdf

Online Tutorials and Courses (on technical and other topics)
www.learnthat.com/computers/

Basic Computer Tutorial
www.comptechdoc.org/basic/basictut/

If any of these websites are not available or you wish to seek out additional information, we encourage you to do your own online search. Consider the concepts covered in the chapter that are most important to you, and think of various terms that could be used to describe them. For this chapter, some potential keywords to search include:

basic computer terms

computer literacy

computer tutorial

When searching online, consider different ways to express ideas. Remember to use synonyms and related words. Try phrasing things in different ways. And always review more than the first few pages of search results.

For more specific information on searching online, refer to Chapter 10.

E-Books: The Evolution of the Textbook

14

Understand the types of e-books.

Understand what is driving the shift to e-books.

Learn how to use your e-book most efficiently.

Recognize the options you have in using e-books.

Power UP

Students want choices. One manner in which publishers and schools have responded to this is by offering e-books. An e-book or electronic book is a new and innovative way to deliver your class materials. However, not only are your class materials being delivered online now—many people are reading novels, magazines, and more in electronic format. Chances are you have already made the transition to reading something online that at one time would only have been available in print, such as a newspaper. You may remember the days of toting heavy backpacks as you made your way to class. Well, the heavy backpack is being displaced by a code to log onto the Internet and download your book online. You may now carry a laptop. Or perhaps you just read your book at home on your home computer. Or better yet, maybe you have some type of handheld device which stores your book. The choices are limitless. So let's talk a little about e-books, what they are, why you may be using them, and how to get the most out of the experience.

TYPES OF E-BOOKS

An e-book, generally speaking, is your class textbook created in an electronic file and made available either for download or for reading online. Sometimes your e-book may also include instructor materials and simulations. For the sake of this discussion, we are focusing on the textbook content.

An e-book can come in many different formats. You might have a simple PDF, or you might have a flash paper. Your e-book could be delivered through various platforms such as VitalSource, CourseSmart, CafeScribe or others. You might be able to download your book, or you may only be able to read it online. It may be offered through a subscription that will eventually expire. The choices and variables are many.

A simple PDF (portable document format) is the most basic format of an e-book. PDFs can be converted to XML or HTML files and used on certain platforms. Publishers use PDFs to print their books, so a PDF file would match a printed book exactly. Since PDFs are portable documents, they can be viewed on most computers and mobile devices with Adobe Reader and Reader X, free applications. A PDF is usually downloadable. But though they are easy to create, PDFs are difficult to protect, so often publishers do not like to offer PDFs as e-books, and for this reason you don't see them used a lot. (By protection we mean, students could print these off and "give away" the content.) Also, a basic PDF does not offer a lot of options to the user in terms of functionality.

A flash paper e-book is a little more sophisticated and dynamic. This type of file usually allows for "page fidelity," which means the book appears online exactly as it would in print—for example, the page numbers are exactly the same. A flash paper may only be available online; however, a flash paper e-book may have extras embedded in it such as videos and links to websites. Turning the page of your e-book is actually seen online as a book with the pages flipping.

The features of an e-book vary depending on the format. Some formats allow you to take notes within the e-book and save these to a printable file. Some types of e-books allow you to take notes to share with other users. You see this feature used often by the instructor, who may make notes pointing out important information in the book. Some e-books even allow you to share notes with other students at other schools.

E-books can be delivered by various platforms. The platform of an e-book is similar to the LMS for a course—it is a way for the publisher to organize and control the content and the viewer to access it.

Your e-book might be delivered in a platform such as VitalSource. VitalSource allows you to build a bookshelf much like iTunes. You are able to download your e-book to two computers. The VitalSource platform also gives you capabilities to add notes or make comments and have an interactive experience with your e-book.

Other popular platforms include CourseSmart and CafeScribe. CourseSmart is a large repository of e-books by several different publishing companies. CourseSmart allows you to access your e-book on one computer. CafeScribe allows for one download to a single computer as well as online access.

Most major publishers have their own platform for e-books—McGraw-Hill has Primis, Wiley has Desktop Editions, Cengage has CengageBrain, Pearson has the Pearson eText. All the different platforms have unique functionality—for instance, the Pearson eText is only available while online and does not allow students to download the book.

Depending on the platform, an e-book may have many features. Some of the most common ones include:

- Note taking
- Highlighting
- Note saving to printable file
- Book sharing
- Word searching
- Downloading
- Online only

 ## E-BOOK ACCESS

How long you have to access an e-book can vary.

Subscriptions to e-books are generally not forever. Typically a subscription will be for 180 days. This is on average how long a student is in class. This means when the class is over, the book is gone. Literally, one day you log into class to access your book and it is no longer available. This ability to delete the book off your computer happens through the digital rights management (DRM) agreement put in place by the publisher. This could be a drawback for you if there is a reason you would like to keep the book. Keep this in mind, because if there is information in the book you think will be useful later in your program, then you will want to explore whether you can ensure that your e-book access will not expire—or buy the hard copy.

As was noted above, your e-book may be accessible only online or it could be downloadable. In some instances, the book might be downloadable but only to a single computer. In other instances, the book might be downloadable to several computers. In yet other instances, your book could reside on an "online bookshelf," and would be accessible to you anytime you are on the Internet. Sometimes you can download the book, or parts of it, to your smartphone.

When you are ready to access your e-book, there are different ways this can be accomplished. Your e-book might be living in your schools' learning management system, or you may need an actual code to download the book from a bookstore or publisher website. If the book is integrated in the school's learning management system, there is a good chance you will only need to sign in and the book will be a click away. However, if you need a code, it is most often ordered through the bookstore and sent to you via the mail, or through the school's e-mail.

All of these parameters—including format of the e-book, delivery platforms, subscription duration, and how you access the book—will be established by either your school or your professor and the publisher prior to the course being made available to you. These parameters are generally not negotiable by you. This means the publisher and the school or professor decide what you are going to get and how it will be set up.

So there is no standard type of e-book you can expect—what type of e-book you get depends on the circumstances. If the individual professor set it up, then you may have to learn an entirely new way of managing your book in the next class. If the school set up the e-books, it may be somewhat easier to get through your classes once you figure out how the e-books work. If not, you will need to experiment until you figure out how to access the books. It is not like grabbing a book off the shelf—the price we pay for having choices is that there is no standard.

WHY E-BOOKS?

If you have had experience using an e-book, you will have your own opinion about them. Perhaps surprisingly, research indicates students do not really like e-books. The hard-copy books we are all familiar with are portable and easy to use. Plus, there just seems to be something indescribable about our partialness to paper books—most people like the feel of the book in their hands or the opportunity to smell the freshness of the paper. But the bottom line is that schools may choose to offer an e-book, and, in some instances only an e-book, for many reasons—cost, availability, or customization. So brace yourself, as the move to e-books seems inevitable. However, this does not have to limit you. You still have choices. Sometimes e-books come with a print-to-order option, or the hard-copy book is still available from the bookstore. There are also some instances where it does not make sense to have or use an e-book. Some subjects and materials just do not work that well in an online file, such as math. It is easier to study your math homework from an actual printed book.

Among the reasons for offering e-books are inventory, accessibility, the dynamic media the e-book offers, transportability, flexibility for instructors, and resource management. With e-books, there is always inventory—no out-of-stock issues and no classes starting without books. With e-books, the publishers do not have to print, warehouse, or ship an actual product. The publisher may still print a code on cardboard stock and send it to the school bookstore. This code gives students access to the e-books; however, more often than not, the e-book is alive and accessible right in the students' online class, and thus there is nothing to ship.

E-books can result in a lot of savings for publishers, which can be passed on to the schools, which ultimately can be passed on to students. This is why e-books are often not nearly as expensive as a hard-copy book.

Another reason to use e-books is accessibility. It is nice to log into class and have your materials waiting there for you—to avoid either waiting for the book to be delivered by mail or making a trek to the local bookstore to purchase it. Depending on the setup, it is possible you could access your book virtually at any time from any location, once you are online.

E-books are sometimes more interactive and engaging. Remember the "old days" when textbooks may have contained a few pictures and a case study at the back of a chapter? In an e-book the case study may be an actual simulation you can interact with, and every picture can be a video. This enhances the learning experience for students, especially if this is important to your learning style.

For students who are visually impaired, e-books can be read to the student more easily. There is software you can purchase that will take the written word and change it to an audio file. This is also an advantage to students who may have an auditory learning style. You could take your e-book and transfer it into an audio file, download it to your iPod, and go off on a run while you listen to your reading materials.

E-books are both more and less transportable. They are more transportable because if you have a portable computer or reader, you can access any number of books through the machine. However, they can also be thought of as less transportable, because you have to have the machine and maybe Internet access. And there are exceptions based on what type of e-book the school and publisher has decided to make available.

For instructors there are lots of reasons to use e-books to enhance the students' learning experience. They can customize their course materials more closely to what they believe the students should be learning in the class. For example, they can use chapters from several different books combined together and placed online. Further, instructors can add their own materials and completely customize the course. This takes learning to a new level. You might argue that this could be done with a print book too, but an e-book allows this to be more dynamic and immediate. Imagine if you were studying economics and your book was an e-book. If there was something happening on a given day that you were currently studying in class, the instructor could go into the e-book and post a note to you to explain how the theory discussed in the book is actually occurring in the real world at that exact moment.

Finally, a great reason to use e-books is the decreased amount of paper and ink waste. We all know there is an initiative to green America and to be conscious of waste. Many organizations are moving to paperless offices. Think about your local doctor's office—often all your medical records are in electronic format. Gone are the days when a manila folder held all the patient information. Now, the doctor comes in with a handheld computer and takes notes. E-books are a direct correlation with this effort.

USING E-BOOKS

So you start a class and log in and realize there is an e-book rather than a print book—what do you do? Well, it depends on many different factors.

As mentioned before, the e-book may be available with just a click of the mouse. Or, it may be you need a code to access the book. If it is your first class using an e-book, you might check with your advisor or faculty member. If you have had previous classes with e-books, chances are the current class and e-book is set up just like the previous classes, so use that model. The way you use your e-book will be different from your print book, and there are some wonderful opportunities only found in e-books, so let's discuss a few of those things.

First, as you are reading the book, you may feel a need to print the book. Keep in mind printing your book can be very costly, as ink and paper are expensive. Plus this really does not help with the efforts to green America, so we encourage you to think seriously about whether or not it is necessary.

If you decide to print and find out you cannot, it may be the way the publisher and your school has set up the e-book. Publishers obviously do not want their intellectual property, the content of the book, out in the open for anyone to print, so they often will limit how many times you can print the book and sometimes they do not allow it at all.

We encourage you to keep a notebook and take notes on the important sections you want to remember. Taking these notes will also reinforce what you are learning. If your book happens to be a flash paper, you may be able to take notes in the book and transport the notes to a different file. Many e-books also have the capability to allow highlighting within the text on-screen. You can save this for ease of use later—when you want to revisit this important information, you simply look for the highlighted sections.

A very useful feature that might be available to you in your e-book is the ability to search for key words. This is helpful if you are studying or writing a paper on a specific topic. If you can remember reading about it, but you cannot remember where, you can very quickly do a search and find the information. This is similar to looking up key words in the index of a book, but not all print books have a thorough index, and this is much easier done online.

In some situations you may have the option to buy an e-book or to buy a print book. There are many factors to consider if given this option. The first question you might consider is, what is the topic of the book? Is this a book you might want to reference later in your program? If so, there is a chance you will want to buy the book to have as a long-term resource.

If you are traveling a lot or you are in the military and living overseas, you might prefer an e-book to avoid the cost of shipping a print book. On the other hand, maybe your connection to the Internet is slow and it would take you a long time to download the book. These are all factors to consider. You will need to analyze the details of your circumstances before you make a decision. Consider cost, access, and functionality, and make the best decision with your learning in mind.

As with so many aspects of technology in our world today, the e-book market is ever changing. There is no standard. It is not like the textbook market, where the biggest decision was whether to have a hard-cover book or soft-cover book. There are many variations and new technologies entering the market all the time. By the time this book publishes, things could be different; however, what we have sought to do in this chapter is give you an idea of the possible features and functionality of an e-book, and how this format might work within your online course. This way, you can make informed decisions and have the best learning environment and opportunity.

MORE POWER TO YOU

Now is your chance to explore this chapter's topics further. Check out the sites listed here. Enjoy expanding your knowledge, and *more power to you*!

What Is All About Ebooks?
www.articlesbase.com/internet-articles/what-is-all-about-ebooks-1425947.html

Frequently Asked Questions about Ebooks and Ereaders
www.bookfinder.com/books/ebooks_faq/

MobileRead Forums > E-Book Readers > Which One Should I Buy?
www.mobileread.com/forums/showthread.php?t=95117

Company Offers College Textbooks for Free
www.cnn.com/2009/TECH/08/21/free.college.textbooks/index.html

If any of these websites are not available or you wish to seek out additional information, we encourage you to do your own online search. Consider the concepts covered in the chapter that are most important to you, and think of various terms that could be used to describe them. For this chapter, some potential keywords to search include:

e-book library

CourseSmart

VitalSource

Pearson eText

CafeScribe

When searching online, consider different ways to express ideas. Remember to use synonyms and related words. Try phrasing things in different ways. And always review more than the first few pages of search results.

For more specific information on searching online, refer to Chapter 10.

Creating the Ideal Personalized Study Environment

15

THE IMPORTANCE OF A PERSONALIZED WORK SPACE

A personalized work space allows you to be more efficient. Maybe you are a completely organized, clean-desk person. Or maybe you prefer to be surrounded by piles of papers. However you work best, try to set up a dedicated work space for doing your class work where you are comfortable both mentally and physically.

Ergonomics

Ergonomics focuses on designing and arranging equipment to accommodate the people who use it. Consider these questions: Is your chair comfortable to sit in for long periods of time? Is your desk at the right level for you to access your work easily from that chair? Is your computer screen bright enough to make reading possible but not so glaring that it strains your eyes? All of these questions are ergonomic concerns regarding your work space.

Ergonomics is a buzzword these days because we have realized the implications of long hours at the computer. Some people are suffering from carpal tunnel syndrome. Others complain of shoulder and neck aches. Perhaps you spend a lot of time on the computer at work, and then you come home to the computer to attend class online. Make sure the items in your work space fit you and are set up to afford you the least amount of strain.

Here are a few aspects of your surroundings to consider in terms of the ergonomics of your work space:

- *Lighting.* You need proper lighting in your work space. You do not want to harm your eyes by putting unnecessary stress on them, so consider purchasing a lamp to sit on your desk. Be sure your office space is in a well-lit place in your home. Check to be sure the brightness of your computer screen is at an optimal level.

- *Seating.* Your chair should allow you to sit in a comfortable, upright position, close enough to your desk or computer to allow easy access. Of course the chair cannot control whether you sit up straight or slouch. We leave that to you.

- *Desk.* Set up the height, space, and organization of items on your desk to make your work easily accessible. You should be able to comfortably fit your legs under the desk while you work.

- *Yourself.* A big part of remaining comfortable and productive depends on your own habits and actions. Remember to sit up straight. Change position occasionally. Breathe! And stand up and stretch every so often.

To find out more about setting up your work space properly, we recommend you search online or at your local library.

The Ideal Study Environment

How often have you thought, "I can't wait to get home and snuggle up in my favorite chair or in my comfy bed." How does that make you feel? Warm, safe, comfortable, and cozy? Now imagine how exciting learning could be if you had that same thought when you were preparing to study: "I cannot wait to go to my learning space and learn." What if the thought of going to a place to study could conjure up real excitement?

It can happen if you make it that way. You can be much more successful if you approach learning with enthusiasm. Your learning space can become a special place for you. Online students have more control over their learning environment because they do not have to go to a stuffy classroom with one-size-fits-all seats and tables. However, this benefit can change to a major drawback if you do not create a pleasant study environment. If set up correctly, your environment can help put you in the proper mood for completing your work.

Too often students comment that they have a laptop, so they can work anywhere. They sit in their comfy chair or take the laptop to bed to work where they fall asleep! Keep in mind that the comfy chair and bed are associated in your mind with relaxation. You do not want to be too relaxed when it comes time to study. Further, sitting and trying to work in an easy chair or the bed does not provide the appropriate ergonomic support.

One of your authors became particularly aware of the importance of a well-organized work space when she visited a friend. The friend's office was brightly lit, with a beautiful cherry desk, a comfortable chair, books, pens, a computer, and a printer. It made her think, "I want to sit down and go to work." It was there that she realized how important a perfect learning environment could be. The moment had a huge impact on her. She went home and began to create her own ideal work space.

We know many of you are on a budget so it may take a while to achieve that perfect space. But once you do, you might rather be in that little area of your home than any other.

Think about what your perfect work space might look like. Consider what you have seen in other people's homes or offices, or in magazines. Ask yourself what you liked and didn't like, and begin to plan where and how you can create your own space.

Study Space in Your Home

Try to avoid setting up your study space anywhere that you will need to vacate later. It is time consuming to move your materials, and then you have to take time to reorganize everything. Every time you move things, you risk losing track of your supplies. In such circumstances your classroom and your work space become transient. At a subconscious level, you might begin to view your education as unstable, too.

We recommend you do not set up your study space in the kitchen, at the dining room table, or the coffee table. Try to find yourself a spot, even if it is a tiny corner in your house or apartment, and make it a permanent home for your schoolwork.

If possible, create your work space where you have a window and a view. Taking a moment to catch your breath and relax is important. Two definite benefits will come from this. First, you will be able to look out and relax; quite often this break will trigger new thoughts. Second, you can open the window and let in some fresh air, which works wonders on a tired brain.

Consider what your perfect work space might look like.

Work-Space Tools

First, you need your computer, and a printer if possible. You also must have your books, including the school-sanctioned writing guide, a dictionary, perhaps a thesaurus, in other words, your resource books. Next you will need writing utensils and papers. You may want a calculator. Paper clips, stapler, and tape are also great additions. Keep in mind that this list is not exhaustive, and most of these items can be purchased locally for a minimal cost.

Furnishing your work space does not have to be expensive. You may find bargains at garage sales, on Craigslist, or at a dollar store. Decorate your area with items that motivate you. Perhaps you want some pictures of people you admire or some quotes that inspire you. Furnish the area with your personality in mind. As you can see, you can put together a nice work space for a very reasonable cost if you open your eyes to the alternatives.

WORKING REMOTELY

One of the perks of online learning is that you are not necessarily limited by location. Especially if you have a laptop computer, you can, for all practical purposes, take the classroom with you.

For some, traveling is not an option; it is a requirement for holding the job that allows them to stay in school. For these students, learning the ropes of going to school while traveling is a necessity. For others, traveling is not required but something that may come up on occasion, and being able to access your class while on the road is a wonderful advantage. However, there are many things to consider and many pitfalls to avoid. As glamorous as it may sound, you may not be at your best when you are crammed into an airport chair, surrounded by people and noise. In addition, not always having the ability to connect to the Internet can be a problem. To be successful, you must be able to connect to class.

If your job calls for travel, you may log in to class from various locations. Even if travel is not required, you still can enjoy the portability of online learning. Airports, libraries, and coffee shops are some of the many places that offer wireless access. To work in any of these off-site locations, be aware of access (open/private), power source, cost, and privacy.

Where to Connect

Knowing where you can obtain Internet access, and knowing it ahead of time, is crucial. Do not assume you are going to be able to obtain wireless access "somewhere" when you travel. In addition, do not count on open access as you travel because remote networks can be notoriously unreliable. Common locations that offer wireless Internet access include the following.

Hotels

Hotels may offer wireless access throughout the property, in the rooms, or through a connection in their "corporate work center." It can be complimentary or for a fee. Some hotels charge up to $15 or more a night for a wireless connection. Numerous hotels, especially in smaller towns, do not offer any access at all.

Airports

Some airports have Internet access and others do not. The access may not be free, and even if it is, it may not be compatible with your system without doing some manipulating. Some airlines are also beginning to offer Internet access inflight, for a fee.

Restaurants

Occasionally you can find a restaurant that offers wireless access. It may be completely free, free with your meal purchase, or available only for a separate fee.

Libraries

Many libraries do offer free Internet access, either through their network or on their local computers. Keep in mind, however, that to access the network, you will usually need a library member card. And when you are not a local resident, it is unlikely you will be able to obtain one.

Coffee Shops

Free access is a possibility. At some places, you can buy a day pass for $10 or so that will allow you to connect in areas where the company who sold you the day pass has service. For example, at a Starbucks, usually you can buy a day pass from T-Mobile for $10, but it will not work at all locations.

Wireless Modems

Often known as aircards or simcards, wireless modems are able to connect just about anywhere, anytime. You simply plug the aircard into your USB port and connect to your provider's network. While this is a very exciting option for students to have, keep in mind it can be expensive. To purchase an aircard, you usually have to spend between $50 and $100 and sign a contract—just like a cell phone. You then have the additional monthly service fee of $50–$75 (prices can vary). You might want to consider checking to see if your company sponsors aircard purchases. An aircard can provide you with a lot of freedom while in school.

A common theme you might notice here is that access can be free, but is not always. If you can find a venue that offers *reliable* free wireless or other access, count yourself lucky.

To work in any of these off-site locations, there are a few additional points to keep in mind. Most places allow you to plug in and not pay for electricity; however, available outlets are usually limited in number and can be hard to locate. The more obvious and accessible they are, the more quickly, and regularly, they will be in use by someone who got there before you. This situation means that you need to have plenty of battery power, and you may want to buy a backup battery.

Privacy

Do not rely on open access as you travel. Remote networks can be notoriously unreliable. Although most of what you are doing is not private, you just never know who is looking in on what you are doing, so it is best to be safe. Most people are not apt to look into your class and steal any information, but you never know. Use a secure connection whenever possible. If that is not an option, work offline until you need to upload or download information.

Other Concerns

Carry, Do Not Check, Your Computer

Plan to carry your laptop with you while you travel. The rough handling it can suffer when loaded as luggage can often result in a crashed hard drive or other damage. And always remember to label it with your name and contact information—not just the case, but the computer itself as well.

Working Offline Between Connections

Some learning platforms allow you to download your messages and work offline. Find out if this is the situation in your class. If you are taking a long plane or car ride, you can use that time to read through class messages you have downloaded. If you cannot download messages, copy and paste as much as possible into Word documents. Then when you are on the plane or in the car, work on those items. This technique makes for an efficient use of time and assures you have what you need to log into class.

Changing Time Zones

Another factor to consider when traveling is the time zone. What time zone is your class in and what time are assignments due? You may have to adjust so you can meet the requirements of class in the usual time zone.

Traveling Abroad

In addition to time zone concerns, traveling abroad brings up entirely different issues. You have to consider that your plugs may not work in the available outlets. Online accessibility may be shaky or nonexistent, depending on your destination. Jet lag and/or the complete unfamiliarity of your surroundings may throw you off in general. You will need to consider all of these possibilities before you leave.

Vacationing

If you think going on vacation and taking your class work with you is a good idea, you might want to reconsider. First, ask yourself if taking class while on vacation really puts you in the right frame of mind to do your best. Usually the point of a vacation is to relax and escape from your everyday concerns and obligations, rather than to focus on doing homework. If you think you will be able to motivate yourself, consider time and access, as well as space in your luggage for the necessary supplies.

Supplies for Working Off-Site

When you prepare to travel with your portable classroom, be sure to pack all necessary items. First and foremost, you will need your power cord! And verify your battery is charged fully before you leave home.

Be sure you have the manual for your computer, at least for the first few trips. If possible, read it through ahead of time and understand if there are any idiosyncrasies about your computer of which you should be aware.

One of your authors remembers when she traveled with her new laptop for the first time. She could not access the Internet. She struggled with it for hours. She called the help line at the hotel, she contacted friends, and, finally, she realized what she needed to do it: turn on her wireless signal receptor. So simple, yet it took a long time to figure out.

What else might you need to pack? If you travel a lot, you might keep a bag packed with writing utensils, paper, sticky notes, paper clips, and so on. You may even consider buying two copies of the resource guide or style manual.

If you only travel on rare occasions, you need to evaluate what you will want to take. This decision will depend on what is going on in your class. If you are traveling and have a term paper due, you will want to take all resource guides and texts associated with the paper.

Planning for Contingencies

Take a few precautions to ensure that your travel does not disrupt your class participation.

- Complete as many assignments as you can before you ever leave home. Then you can participate or submit the work while you are in transit.

- Be sure you have written down the school's telephone number and your instructor's telephone number, just in case you need it.

- If you reach your destination and your computer will not work or you cannot connect to the Internet, call the school and let the people who matter know what is going on. That usually means your faculty member, and possibly your advisor or team members. Keep the lines of communication open. You are probably not going to be out of commission for an extended period, but be prepared for contingencies.

Overall, the picture we have tried to paint here is this: Traveling while attending school is possible and sometimes necessary. But by no means is it easy, and, honestly, we do not recommend it. We hear numerous complaints from students about the difficulties of trying to stay on top of class work while traveling:

- How they expected to work on their computer during a long flight, but the environment and space issues made it impossible.

- How they could not find the time to complete their schoolwork.

- How trying to connect to the Internet using alternative methods was difficult or impossible.

- How hard it is to know what you will need when you are away, until it is too late.

Think about how time-pressured you are when you travel. The stress of putting yourself in this situation is usually not worth it. Of course, you will be in your program a long time, and traveling is probably inevitable at some point. So before you leave, arm yourself with our tips and, most importantly, have a backup plan.

Do not let this section alarm you. If you have to travel and study, you can do it, but it will require extra planning and negotiation.

MORE POWER
TO YOU

Now is your chance to explore this chapter's topics further. Check out the sites listed here. Enjoy expanding your knowledge and *more power to you*!

UCLA Ergonomics
www.ergonomics.ucla.edu/

Ergo Tips
http://ergo.human.cornell.edu/cuergotipsintro.html

The Study Spot
http://distancelearn.about.com/od/managingyourwork/a/studyspot.htm

OSHA Workstation Checklist
www.osha.gov/SLTC/etools/computerworkstations/index.html

If any of these websites are not available or you wish to seek out additional information, we encourage you to do your own online search. Consider the concepts covered in the chapter that are most important to you, and think of various terms that could be used to describe them. For this chapter, some potential keywords to search include:

   ergonomics

   keyboard yoga

   working remotely

   wireless access tips

When searching online, consider different ways to express ideas. Remember to use synonyms and related words. Try phrasing things in different ways. And always review more than the first few pages of search results.

For more specific information on searching online, refer to Chapter 10.

Preparing for the First Day of Class

16

Power UP

Enjoy the journey of education.

Prepare for the first day of class, both mentally and physically. Use both your excitement and anxiety as motivators. Get involved in your classes. Record your feelings and/or share them with others.

Be proactive the first day of class. Ensure that you have the required textbooks and materials. Check into your class and figure out what you need to do. Post a personal biography. Review the syllabus and assignments. Complete the initial readings and assignments.

Print out the syllabus. You will reference it throughout the course.

Consider carefully which course documents make sense to print out, what makes sense to save to your computer, and what you can leave in the course system to reference later.

The first day of school has finally arrived. The apprehension and excitement that have led up to this day may have been overwhelming, but now it is here. It may seem strange for an online student because there is not a lot of formality. On the surface, life may not seem as though it has changed much, especially for those around you. You do not have to get in your car and drive to class. You do not have to be somewhere at a particular time. But the train has started, and you want to be on board and not get left behind.

In this chapter, we discuss how to prepare for the beginning of school. The main message we would like to communicate to you here is to *enjoy the journey of education*!

RIDING THE WAVE OF EMOTION

One of the authors remembers when she first started her program: She was sitting in her chair drinking coffee and thinking, "It is the first day of school." To her, things felt different. It is hard to explain, but she knew things were changing. To her family, however, it was just a typical day. She did not leave and go to class. She just spent a bit more time on the computer that day. She still thinks about that feeling and loves it. She was so excited and scared, and she thought, "I just have to complete a class at a time and someday I will be finished."

As you begin school, you will have a lot of feelings. You may feel nervous, excited, intimidated, anxious, and probably proud most of all. To begin acquiring an education is a very important step. Your entire world is about to change.

At a college orientation, a professor said that a parent of a graduate mentioned her daughter had completely changed during the years in school. To that, the professor replied, "Good, that is what is supposed to happen." The professor went on to explain that, if the school had not changed the student, the school would not have met its requirements and obligations to the student and her family.

Your school has the same obligation to you. The classes you take should help you grow and develop as a person. Not only will you gain new knowledge, skills, and perspectives, but you will also develop new relationships.

Let's talk about your feelings. First, you will be nervous, which is normal. You do not know what to expect and you wonder if you can live up to the commitments. The answer is, *Yes, you can.* Keep in mind that everyone in the class, and possibly even the instructor, is feeling the same way. It is normal to be apprehensive. Try to use this anxiety positively. Let it motivate and inspire you to plan and get organized for class. Use it as an impetus to catapult yourself into success, rather than letting it be a negative influence.

You are probably excited, too. You may have thought about and dreamed about this undertaking for a long time. Now the time is here. Try to capture some of this excitement using a journal. It may benefit you to remember this feeling later in the program, if and when the going becomes rough. Excitement is wonderful, so enjoy it and share it with others. You may be surprised to find that your feelings about furthering your education can inspire others to take on the same challenges—perhaps your friends or your children. When they see how much you are looking forward to taking this step, it can lead them to think about their own educational choices.

You are probably intimidated as well. Everyone probably feels this way when they are in unknown territory. Do not think you are the only one. You can manage your intimidation by taking a deep breath and becoming more involved. Force yourself to engage and to put new ideas and thoughts out there. School should be a safe environment to try new things. Take advantage of it. Talk about your ideas and let others respond. You are here to grow. Part of that growth is learning how to manage all these feelings successfully.

Finally, as mentioned earlier, you are probably very proud. You are a student! You are on the way to earning your degree. Just to be taking on this challenge is a great achievement. Enjoy this time and bask in the joy of being a student.

Keep in mind what you are feeling is no different than the others in the class, so you all have this in common. You might want to share your feelings with the other students and the instructor.

ACTUAL PREPARATIONS

You have sorted out your feelings, and now it is time to begin. You will want to plan for acquiring your books and orienting yourself in your online classroom(s).

Textbooks

First, you want to ensure you have the required textbooks for your classes. Most courses have one or two books, but on occasion you may take a class that requires more. Or you may have one that uses no books and only relies on research and online readings. Although more schools are turning to e-books all the time, it is still the norm in the majority of courses that hard-copy textbooks are the main instructional material. As mentioned in Chapter 14, even if your school is using an e-book, you can often opt for a hard-copy book if you prefer.

Obviously, you first need to find out what the required materials are and how you are expected to acquire them:

- Does the school have an online bookstore where you can order your materials?
- Will you need to open an account with the school bookstore for the duration of your program?
- Are your materials e-books or hard-copy books? If e-books, refer to Chapter 14.
- Unless you are going to buy them from a local store, what is the average timeline for delivery? In other words, how soon can you expect to receive your books after you place the order?

Acting fast is wise because sometimes books can be back-ordered or there are delivery issues. By ordering your course materials as soon as possible, you can alleviate or avoid problems. Having the right books for your course, on time, will help you be successful.

If you do not have your books by the first day of class, you are not going to start off on the best foot. So acquire them as soon as they are identified for you.

Do *not* think you can make your way through a class without completing the required readings; you cannot. Your textbooks are a necessary expense, and you will incur these costs throughout your program, so plan for it.

Buying Used Books

You might be thinking you will purchase used books to save some money. Before you do that, however, do some research to make sure used materials will serve your needs adequately.

In some cases, you can acquire a used book that is exactly the same as the new version you would buy, and it is indeed a better deal. In other cases, you must buy the new version of the text. To know whether a used book is indeed a wise buy, ask a few questions:

- Is the used book *exactly the same edition* as the required book for the course? Do the ISBNs match?
- What condition is the used book in? Is it missing any pages? Does it have highlighting or margin notes from the previous owner that will disrupt your own readings?

- Were there any supplements, such as CDs, DVDs, guidebooks, or access codes for websites, that came with the original book? Are these included with the used book?

Check out all these factors before you decide to buy used books.

Orienting Yourself Online

The Biography (Bio)

You will want to check into your class and figure out what you need to do. Quite often the first task is to post a personal biography. You may want to write a standard bio and keep it. Save it to a file, so you can use it for every class.

- Emphasize professional and perhaps previous school experience.
- Keep your bio short and succinct. If your bio is too long, you risk the chance others will find it boring and thus not read it at all.
- Steer away from providing too much personal information. You are introducing yourself to strangers for the first time, not posting your life story. Do not view your bio as an opportunity to "sit on the psychiatrist's couch." You definitely should not post your phone number and address. You can probably trust everyone in your class, but you can never be too careful.

Create a bio with relevant information that another student and faculty member would want to read about you. This is not a forum for divulging your innermost thoughts. As other students post their bios, you may want to comment and look for things you have in common. Responding is a great way to connect with other students and begin creating a learning community. Remember, the bio exchange is the introduction to the class.

The Syllabus

After you post your bio and begin to look around in the class space for course materials, seek out the syllabus and assignments. A *syllabus* is an outline of assignments in the class and their due dates. Think of the syllabus as your bible. You should study the syllabus, learn the syllabus, and love the syllabus, and we are going to explain why.

First, keep in mind that the syllabus can be overwhelming if you look at all the assignments and think you have to do all of them *today*. You will do a little at a time, a bit each day, building toward the finish of the course. Do not be overwhelmed. Keep it in perspective.

Look at the syllabus and understand the policies unique to your instructor and what he or she thinks is most important. Some faculty members emphasize participation; some emphasize the format of the paper; the instructor's priority, whatever it is, should be stated in the syllabus, although it is not always obvious. You may have to review the entire document to find it.

Consider what is worth the most points in the class, and focus on those assignments. If you have a project worth 20% of the course grade, you will want to spend the most time with that assignment. If you have an assignment worth only 5% and you find you have to miss something, that would be the assignment to miss.

It is all about strategy and figuring out what can give and what cannot. Certainly we do not advocate ever missing assignments, which not only hurts your grade, but also affects your learning. However, you are a working adult with commitments and may have to let something go. If you do, it is good to know ahead of time where the leeway is.

Make sure you understand due dates, which can be tricky in an online environment because of the time zones. Some schools require that assignments be posted by the time zone where the server is, usually at the corporate headquarters of the school. Others require that assignments be submitted by the student's time zone. Yet others require the assignment be due by the faculty member's time zone.

Due dates and times vary with each course, so make sure you are clear on them. Often there is a penalty for a late submission, and these penalties can add up quickly. Do not fall victim to this. Submitting work late can hurt your grade in no time at all. If you find yourself in a situation where you are unable to submit your assignment on time, find out how late an assignment can be. Even if you submit the assignment late, you may be able to earn some points, and some points are better than none.

Completing Assignments

After you have reviewed the syllabus and completely understand the requirements, begin to answer any questions posted for the class discussion, and complete your readings and assignments. Making a good first impression with both the instructor and fellow learners is important. Do this by posting answers to the questions that are complete and thoughtful, not too wordy, yet add to the conversations.

Oftentimes students comment that answering the same discussion question as all the other students is difficult because the others have already "captured the answer." Here are a few suggestions:

- Be the first one to answer the question.
- Do not read the other students' answers until you post yours.
- Read all of the other students' messages, research the topic, and then provide a completely different viewpoint.
- Connect the question with real life by detailing your answer with relevant information from your own life experiences or issues in the news or pop culture.

Doing assignments online is no different than doing assignments for an on-ground class. These assignments generally require the same attention and detail. Consider how much latitude you have regarding the assignments. If possible, double-dip. In other words, arrange it so an assignment for class also serves a purpose for your job. Or if you happen to be taking two classes, do an assignment that applies to both classes. This takes a lot of preplanning and thought, but being efficient in this way can help save you time in the long run. Considering alternate applications of course topics also helps you retain that information.

If you are highly scheduled and like to see when you can complete obligations by mapping it out, you might print out a calendar of due dates. Then you can personalize it with actual days and times you know you will have open to work on the different assignments.

CLASS GETS UNDER WAY

You posted your bio, you studied the syllabus, and you have a plan/strategy to be a success. You will need to continue to focus on other elements of managing the class. Knowing what resources to have available is helpful. Sometimes it varies by class.

Determining What to Print

Too often, students think they need to print every document for the class. Perhaps you really need the printed documents, but think it through beforehand.

The one document you should definitely print is the syllabus. And if there is a class calendar, print that too. However, as far as the other documents, it is quite possible you will not need to print them. Printing too many materials can cause you problems:

- In determining which ones are really important for continued reference
- In having documents cluttering your office
- In having a printer that is constantly out of ink

You have to print what you need to be comfortable, but before you go crazy printing everything, really ask yourself if you need it or if it is something you could look up again later in the electronic environment. How much you need to print will vary by class. For example, in a quantitative class, you may print more materials than you would in an English class because you may have to work out the equations, samples, and so on. However, one could argue that in an English class, you may want to edit your paper using a pen and paper. For each new circumstance, you will need to reconsider what makes sense to print.

A viable alternative to printing materials is to save the documents to your desktop for easy retrieval. Save the key documents, and if you end up referring to them regularly, print them out. If you do not refer to them often, then just having them readily available on your machine may be enough.

Now you have started your class. You know what is going on and you know the commitments, but perhaps others do not. Think about sharing your experience with them. Be sure to include them in your world; the more they understand, the more likely they will be there to support you.

We encourage you to journal your feelings as you begin class. Never forget that excitement you feel. Remembering this feeling will help you become reenergized as you become discouraged or tired. And you will. The key will be to keep going even after that excitement wears off.

MORE POWER TO YOU

Now is your chance to explore this chapter's topics further. Check out the sites listed here. Enjoy expanding your knowledge and *more power to you*!

Preparing for Classroom Learning
www.studygs.net/classrm.htm

Influencing Teachers
www.studygs.net/attmot2.htm

Be Proactive
www.stevepavlina.com/blog/2004/11/be-proactive/

If any of these websites are not available or you wish to seek out additional information, we encourage you to do your own online search. Consider the concepts covered in the chapter that are most important to you, and think of various terms that could be used to describe them. For this chapter, some potential keywords to search include:

preparing online class

online student resources

When searching online, consider different ways to express ideas. Remember to use synonyms and related words. Try phrasing things in different ways. And always review more than the first few pages of search results.

For more specific information on searching online, refer to Chapter 10.

Maintaining Your Online Success

17

Power UP

- Set up a filing system to organize important course documents. Staying organized will help you stay efficient.

- Take steps to prepare for the next class. Find out what you need to do to enroll. Order your books and materials early.

- Plan for contingencies. Be prepared for emergencies or the unexpected. Back up your files regularly, either electronically or with hard copies.

- Think twice before you discard books. The books from previous classes can provide resource material in subsequent courses. They can also become valuable references beyond your academic career.

- Take time to relax and enjoy the reprieve if you have a break between classes. But do not become too comfortable or you may not want to go back to school.

- Remember that each instructor and each course will be different. Learn from your past experiences, but be open-minded about the future.

- Reward yourself for a great accomplishment. Acknowledge your continued success as you finish each class.

- Maintain a positive outlook. Cultivate your belief in yourself and your potential for success.

In closing, we talk about continuing your education. You will see that beginning is easy. You have heard people talk about the "honeymoon period" or how the "newness wears off," and these stages may apply to you as you go through your program.

When you begin school, you will be full of excitement and drive, and that alone can keep you going for the first few classes. But the truth is, at some point in your program you may feel down and discouraged about how much more there is to do. You may wonder if it is all worth it, and you may even consider not continuing. This chapter addresses what it takes to maintain your online success and continue when you feel like hanging it up.

STAYING ORGANIZED

As you progress through the program and each class, your knowledge will grow. But so will the number of textbooks and electronic documents you have to keep track of. Staying organized will help you stay efficient.

Computer Files

We suggest you set up a filing system to store important documents. You may choose to use a hard-copy filing system, but we recommend that you save work on the computer as much as you can. It will save both space and paper.

Use your desktop and create folders. Ideally you have a folder for each class, and in that folder you store all the documents you created for the class.

Take the time to develop your own logical system of filing. Be sure you use brief but descriptive names for all your documents, and perhaps numbers when it is called for. Logical naming of folders helps you easily determine their content after the memory of the particular assignment has faded. The first time you do a large paper with multiple drafts, you will be glad you chose a relevant title for the document and saved the versions using numbers 1 to 4.

You may not see the need for multiple files at first, but as work piles up, you will wish you had it carefully marked and stored. It will make locating the files in the future so much simpler.

We suggest you keep everything: your assignments, your in-depth posts, your answers to discussion questions. You cannot be sure now what may come in handy later. You may be able to build on what you have done for future assignments and posts. For example, if you decide in your business program to focus your papers on Wal-Mart, you could use the same introduction with the company history for each paper. You may also find other bits of information you could reuse.

Textbooks for Future Reference

When you finish a class, you may be tempted to sell your books. There may be compelling reasons to do so. Perhaps you need the money or they take up too much space. However, keep in mind that you are in an academic program and the concepts and ideas will often be related or build on one another. You may find the books from previous classes useful for resource material. By continuing to use your books as references, you reinforce your memory about the concepts you learned in those classes.

You may also discover that certain books can become valuable references well beyond your academic career: You might talk to people who work in your chosen field to find out what books they have found helpful in their work. All of your textbooks might not be worthy of becoming lifetime references. But consider which ones might, and keep them on hand.

If all or some of your course texts are e-books though, you may not have the option of keeping them. Refer to Chapter 14 for more information on e-books.

Emergency Backup

As you progress through the program, always have a plan to back up your work. You need to consider what would happen if your computer were to crash or be infected with a destructive virus, or if a natural disaster occurred.

We all know that computers are not completely reliable. *We strongly recommend that you back up your documents periodically.* You could do this by:

- Using a whole drive designed specifically for the purpose.
- Using a small portable thumb or flash drive.
- Saving documents on backup disks.
- Printing hard copies and keeping them in a safe place.
- E-mailing copies to an alternative e-mail account.

If you use a machine backup, make sure the backup system itself contains enough memory to hold everything you need to save.

Whichever option you choose, back up regularly. Weekly is usually good, and daily is better. This kind of planning is easy to dismiss or overlook but can save your sanity, if not your life.

You will work hard completing assignments as you move through your program. Do not let some unforeseen glitch cause your hard work to be lost.

THE MASTER JUGGLER: YOU

You will have so much to manage while you are completing your academic program. Acquiring an education while working and trying to stay involved with family and friends is a juggling act. You will find yourself trying to figure out what you can give up and what you must maintain in order to survive.

Planning Ahead

You will always need to be looking ahead and calculating your time constraints and how they can be managed. For example, if you have children and they are out of school for the summer, you may not want to take a challenging class at that time. You might want to wait until the fall when everyone's lives are more structured. It may be easier then for you to fit in more time for class.

The holidays can also lead to increased stress. You are busy in school as well as trying to step up to all the commitments that come along with the holidays: social obligations, family gatherings, and shopping, for example. As you select your courses and plan your schedule for the semesters ahead, be sure to consider all the possible factors that can make demands on your time.

One of your authors remembers some of the conflicts between family and school. In particular, she recalls how classes fell during a few holiday seasons. She once had a class that ended December 23, the day before Christmas Eve. She had a huge paper due. She had to finish it because the policy at the school was that all assignments had to be in when the class ended. It was stressful, but it was worth it to be done before the festivities started.

Another year, she had an assignment due, but the class was not ending; it would continue after a two-week break over Christmas. She ended up submitting the assignment late and taking a hit on the points, but she was okay with that because it was more important for her to be sane and available for her family over the holidays.

As you can see, it is a matter of give and take, determining what is best for each situation and adapting to the circumstances. Strategize for success and determine what will work for you at any given point.

One Class Follows Another and Another

As you are nearing the end of your first class, in fact, any time you are nearing the end of a class, consider what you need to do to prepare for the next class.

What are the enrollment policies at your institution? You will need to find out whether you are automatically enrolled in your next class or whether you are responsible for enrolling yourself.

You will need to know what materials are required. As we have already advised, order your books early, so you can begin working on the next class as soon as possible.

If you have a break between classes, take time to relax and enjoy the reprieve, but do not become too comfortable or you may not want to go back to school.

Studies show the longer you are away from school, the harder it will be to go back. If you are concerned about that, gather your books and start reading and preparing for the next class. Get a jump start on it! As you finish one class and close that door, remember you are starting from square one again in your next class. You have to study the syllabus. You have to learn the faculty member's idiosyncrasies. It is up to you whether you make the same mistakes or learn from your past experiences in subsequent classes. Remember, each instructor is different, so do not expect things to play out as they have before. Adaptability and an open mind are key characteristics to cultivate as you progress through your program.

You can reward yourself for your success in small ways.

Celebrate Your Achievements

As you finish a class, reward yourself for a great accomplishment. If you can afford to take yourself out to lunch or dinner, that's great. But if all you can do is reach your own arm around to pat yourself on the back, then that's enough. Acknowledge your continued success. You deserve it. Do not forget and let it slide. Do not undermine the importance of a reward.

One student we know told us that every time she finished a class, she and her husband would go to happy hour for a cold beer and chicken wings. It was her little treat for a job completed. Plus, it allowed her time to reconnect with her husband before jumping into the next class. Do not overlook the importance of taking the time to appreciate your own effort and sharing your success with those close to you.

 # GOOD-BYE AND GOOD LUCK

This book has been filled with tips. We do not think it covers everything at all. We continue to learn and to think of new ideas.

Online learning is dynamic, which makes creating tips for this environment ever challenging. You will learn new ideas and apply different strategies as you progress through the program, which is what will make you successful. Each of us has to discover our own recipe for success.

Further, we live in an ever-changing landscape: of technology, of obligations, and of individual circumstances. So we have to be flexible and remember what worked at one point in our life may not work at another point, even with school.

You will probably be in school for two years or more. Children will get older, jobs may come and go, you will have both happy and sad times, and through it all, school will go on. You have to stay flexible and figure out how to accomplish your goals. Just as a tree bends in the wind, you will become a stronger and better person for the experience of completing your degree.

Following are some closing thoughts for your education. What can you add?

- Going to school is not easy, but it should be invigorating. You should be excited.

- Keep a journal and record your thoughts when you finish a class. When you feel down, read those thoughts and remind yourself why you are doing this.

- You are worthy of this experience. You have made some sacrifices, and there are more to come, but you will emerge a better person: more experienced, more educated, more confident. Surround yourself with supportive people who will be there just to listen and encourage you.

- Work hard, but remember, you have a life, too. Do not neglect yourself or the special people in your world. Strive for balance.

- Be a good listener, ask questions, and keep an open mind. Stick to your goals, and do not be afraid of failure. Sometimes it can teach you as much, if not more, than success.

- Always enjoy the education. Worry less about the final product, and enjoy the new ideas, concepts, and people that you are being introduced to through your classes.

- *Appreciate the journey.* Believe in yourself and believe in your potential for success. We do!

We hope we have confirmed your desire to attend school online and perhaps even made it stronger. Going to school is both a privilege and the opportunity of a lifetime. We wish you the best!

MORE POWER
TO YOU

Now is your chance to explore this chapter's topics further. Check out the sites listed here. Enjoy expanding your knowledge and *more power to you!*

17 Ways to Reward Yourself
www.weightwatchers.com/util/art/index_art.aspx?tabnum=1&art_id=1911

Six Tips to Earning More Money after Graduation
www.associatedcontent.com/article/184544/five_tips_for_earning_more_money_after
.html

5 Ways for Distance Learners to Stay Motivated
http://distancelearn.about.com/od/managingyourwork/a/motivation.htm

If any of these websites are not available or you wish to seek out additional information, we encourage you to do your own online search. Consider the concepts covered in the chapter that are most important to you, and think of various keywords that could be used to describe them. For this chapter, some potential terms to search include:

organizing computer files

lifelong learner

When searching online, consider different ways to express ideas. Remember to use synonyms and related words. Try phrasing things in different ways. And always review more than the first few pages of search results.

For more specific information on searching online, refer to Chapter 10.

FINANCING YOUR EDUCATION

Many schools offer financial aid. Usually if a school is accredited, it can offer financial aid, which comes in the forms of grants, loans, and scholarships. Do not be shy or reserved about seeking help financially. It is there for you.

This appendix only touches on the vast subject of financial aid. We are not experts on this subject and would not want to lead you astray, but we do think it is important to introduce you to the basics.

Grants are often awarded to students who are in dire need of financial help. Grants are given by the government, and you are not required to pay the money back.

Financial aid can be given based on two factors. Need-based financial aid is for those who meet certain criteria that show they are unable to pay for school on their own. Non-need-based financial aid is available to students who choose to finance their education rather than pay for it up front. All financial aid must be paid back; however, the type you qualify for will determine if you will accumulate interest while in the program as well as when you will begin repayment. Some loans do not accumulate interest; others do. Some require that you pay them back immediately when graduating; others recognize a 6-month grace period. Check with your financial aid officer and find out what you qualify for and what would work for you. Note that a number of private banks lend money for school. Government entities used to provide financial aid in the form of loans, but that is not the case anymore.

Be careful about overextending on financial aid. You do have to pay it back, and although you will graduate and be earning more money, you do not want to devote all of your earnings to repaying loans.

Scholarships are another great way to finance your education. Do not think scholarships are only available to students just graduating or students not in your situation. Check with your financial aid office for scholarship information and also search online.

Scholarships are often awarded by companies, charities, and small interest groups. Scholarships are not paid back. It is your money to use for education. Often you have to apply for the scholarship and may be required to fulfill an obligation such as write a paper, but that is well worth it.

Financial aid usually requires that you maintain a certain grade-point average to continue to qualify and that you stay in class, making progress toward your ultimate goal of graduating. Check what the requirements are so you can make sure you do not lose your funding.

UNDERSTANDING THE IMPORTANCE OF ACCREDITATION

The purpose of accreditation in higher education is to provide a professional review of the quality of an educational program. The U.S. Department of Education is the entity that establishes accreditation policies and accredits institutions. When a school seeks accreditation for its programs, it is opting to have the quality of its program compared with established national or regional standards.

Institutions can be regionally or nationally accredited. Individual educational programs offered at schools can often be programmatically accredited.

Benefits of Accreditation

To receive federal grants and loans, students must attend an accredited university. If you are not sure which school/program is best for you, narrow down the search and be assured of a higher quality program by looking at accredited schools. Further, employers frequently ask if a college or university is accredited before deciding to provide tuition assistance to current employees, and when evaluating the qualifications of new employees.

If you wish to transfer credits seamlessly from one institution to another, having credits from an accredited university is key. At an accredited school, the faculty and staff are involved in evaluating the quality of the instruction and the end-product curriculum, which helps ensure a holistic review of a program.

To learn more about accreditation, visit the following website: www2.ed.gov/admins/finaid/accred/index.html

Allen, E & Seaman, J. (2010). Class differences: Online education in the United States. Babson Research Group.

Allen, I., Garrett, R., and Seaman, J. (2007). Blending in: The extent and promise of blended education in the United States. Retrieved March 5, 2011, from http://sloanconsortium.org/sites/default/files/Blending_In.pdf

American Library Association. (1998). Information literacy defined. Retrieved March 5, 2011, from http://www.ala.org/ala/mgrps/divs/acrl/standards/informationliteracycompetency.cfm#ildef

Annetta, L. (2006). Serious games: Incorporating videogames in the classroom. Retrieved November 23, 2010, from http://net.educause.edu/ir/library/pdf/eqm0633.pdf

Baikie, K., and Wilhelm, K. (2005). Emotional and physical health benefits of expressive writing. *Advances in Psychiatric Treatment, 11*, 338–346. Retrieved August 23, 2007, from http://apt.rcpsych.org/cgi/content/abstract/11/5/338

Betts, K. (2010, Winter). Online Education: Meeting Educational and Workforce Needs through Flexible and Quality Degree Programs. Retrieved May 18, 2011 from http://www.ijournalccc.com/articles/issue_24/betts-lynch.html

Brown, M., and Diaz, V. (2010). Blended learning: A report on the ELI focus session. Retrieved March 5, 2011, from http://net.educause.edu/ir/library/pdf/ELI3023.pdf

Bureau of Labor Statistics. (1999). 1999 Education requirements and job growth. Retrieved December 9, 2004, from http://www.bls.gov/opub/ted/1999/Dec/wk1/art02.htm

Bureau of Labor Statistics. (2004). Projected employment in high-paying occupations requiring a bachelor's or graduate degree. Retrieved March 12, 2005, from http://www.bls.gov/opub/ted/2004/mar/wk3/art03.htm

Bureau of Labor Statistics. (2011), Introduction, p. 20. http://www.bls.gov

Carnevale, D. (2005). Employers still prefer traditional degrees over online learning, study finds. *The Chronicle of Higher Education, 52* (5), A43.

Center for Media Literacy. *Vision & Mission*. Retrieved March 5, 2011, from http://www.medialit.org/about-cml

Dictionary.com Unabridged. (vol. 1.1). (2007). Random House, Inc. Retrieved June 3, 2007, from http://dictionary.reference.com/browse/plagiarism

Framework for 21st Century Learning. (2004). Retrieved November, 23, 2010, from http://www.p21.org/index.php?option=com_content&task=view&id=254&Itemid=120

Gardner, H. (1983). *Frames of mind: The theory of multiple intelligences*. New York: Basic Books.

Gross, R. (1999). *Peak learning*. New York: Tarcher/Penguin.

Hamner, W., and Harnett, D. (1974). Goal setting, performance, and satisfaction in an interdependent task. *Organizational Behavior and Human Performance, 12*, 217–230.

Hill, L. (2001). Learning styles: An examination of learning styles and my personal discovery of my own. Retrieved June 6, 2007, from http://www.authorsden.com/visit/viewarticle.asp?id=1421

IES National Center for Education Statistics—Fast Facts. (n.d.). Retrieved March 5, 2011, from http://nces.ed.gov/fastfacts/display.asp?id=80

Internet Tutorials: Boolean searching on the Internet: A primer in Boolean logic. (n.d.). Retrieved August 23, 2007, from http://www.internettutorials.net/boolean.html

Kerka, S. (1996). Journal Writing and Adult Learning. ERIC Digest No. 174. ERIC Clearinghouse on Adult Career and Vocational Education. Retrieved August 23, 2007, from http://www.ericdigests.org/1997–2/journal.htm

Locke, E. (1968). Towards a theory of task motivation and incentives. *Organizational Behavior and Human Performance, 3*, 157–189.

Myers & Briggs Foundation. (n.d.). Retrieved June 3, 2007, from http://www.myersbriggs.org

Nagel, D. (2010). The future of e-learning is more growth. *The Journal*. Retrieved February 26, 2011 from http://thejournal.com/articles/2010/03/03/the-future-of-e-learning-is-more-growth.aspx

Nagel, D. (2011). Online learning set for explosive growth as traditional classrooms decline. Retrieved February 27, 2011, from http://campustechnology.com/articles/2011/01/26/online-learning-set-for-explosive-growth-as-traditional-classrooms-decline.aspx

Nagel, D. (2010). The future of e-learning is more growth. *The Journal*. Retrieved February 26, 2011 from http://thejournal.com/articles/2010/03/03/the-future-of-e-learning-is-more-growth.aspx

National Center for Education Statistics. (n.d.). Retrieved June 15, 2007, from http://nces.ed.gov

Ragan, L. Best practices in online teaching—pulling it all together—teaching blended learning courses. Retrieved March 5, 2011, from http://cnx.org/content/m15048/latest/

Rhodes, J. (1998). Vision, reading, and computer uses: An interview with distinguished optometrists. Retrieved June 25, 2007, from http://webword.com/interviews/williams.html

Rowland, G., Lederhouse, A., and Satterfield, D. (2004). Powerful learning experiences within coherent learner groups. *Performance Improvement Quarterly, 17* (2), 46–65. Retrieved June 15, 2007, from ProQuest. http://onlinelibrary.wiley.com/doi/10.1111/j.1937–8327.2004.tb00307.x/abstract

The Sloan Consortium. (2007). Retrieved June 15, 2007, from http://www.sloan-c.org *Trends in blended learning research report 2006*. (2006). Retrieved March 5, 2011, from http://www.elearningguild.com/research/archives/index.cfm?id=102&action=viewonly

Using wildcards. (n.d.). Retrieved June 15, 2007, from http://apps.caes.uga.edu/impact/searchhelp.cfm

On the following pages are two signs you can tear out and hang on your door or office space when you are studying and/or testing. Oftentimes the people in our lives need to be reminded that we need our quiet time. We have found this technique to be useful to avoid distractions while studying.

DO NOT DISTURB:
STUDENT STUDYING

DO NOT DISTURB:
STUDENT TESTING

ADDITIONAL GOAL WORKSHEETS

Below are some additional goal worksheets you can use in conjuction with the instructions in Chapter Three to write out additional goals.

Goal:

Specific:

Measurable:

Attainable:

Realistic:

Timely:

Goal:

Specific:

Measurable:

Attainable:

Realistic:

Timely:

Goal:

Specific:

Measurable:

Attainable:

Realistic:

Timely:

Goal:

Specific:

Measurable:

Attainable:

Realistic:

Timely:

Goal:

Specific:

Measurable:

Attainable:

Realistic:

Timely:

Goal:

Specific:

Measurable:

Attainable:

Realistic:

Timely:

Goal:

Specific:

Measurable:

Attainable:

Realistic:

Timely:

TIME MANAGEMENT LOG

Day One

Using the following Time Management Log, record daily activities for the next two days of the work week and analyze if you used your time effectively.

Name:_____ Day: _____

TIME	ACTIVITIES	COMMENTS WAS THIS A GOOD USE OF YOUR TIME? WHY OR WHY NOT? WHAT CAN YOU DO TO USE THIS HOUR MORE EFFECTIVELY?
6:00 a.m.		
7:00 a.m.		
8:00 a.m.		
9:00 a.m.		
10:00 a.m.		
11:00 a.m.		
12:00 p.m.		
1:00 p.m.		
2:00 p.m.		
3:00 p.m.		
4:00 p.m.		
5:00 p.m.		
6:00 p.m.		
7:00 p.m.		
8:00 p.m.		
9:00 p.m.		
10:00 p.m.		
11:00 p.m.		
12:00 a.m.		

TIME MANAGEMENT LOG

Day Two

Using the following Time Management Log, record daily activities for the next two days of the work week and analyze if you used your time effectively.

Name:_____ Day: _____

TIME	ACTIVITIES	COMMENTS WAS THIS A GOOD USE OF YOUR TIME? WHY OR WHY NOT? WHAT CAN YOU DO TO USE THIS HOUR MORE EFFECTIVELY?
6:00 a.m.		
7:00 a.m.		
8:00 a.m.		
9:00 a.m.		
10:00 a.m.		
11:00 a.m.		
12:00 p.m.		
1:00 p.m.		
2:00 p.m.		
3:00 p.m.		
4:00 p.m.		
5:00 p.m.		
6:00 p.m.		
7:00 p.m.		
8:00 p.m.		
9:00 p.m.		
10:00 p.m.		
11:00 p.m.		
12:00 a.m.		

NOTES

NOTES

NOTES

NOTES

NOTES